GROWING UP
ON THE
GRIDIRON

GROWING UP ON THE GRIDIRON

FOOTBALL, FRIENDSHIP, AND THE TRAGIC LIFE OF OWEN THOMAS

VICKI MAYK

BEACON PRESS
BOSTON

BEACON PRESS
Boston, Massachusetts
www.beacon.org

Beacon Press books
are published under the auspices of
the Unitarian Universalist Association of Congregations.

23 22 21 20   8 7 6 5 4 3 2 1

This book is printed on acid-free paper that meets the uncoated paper
ANSI/NISO specifications for permanence as revised in 1992.

Text design and composition by Kim Arney

Library of Congress Cataloging-in-Publication Data

Names: Mayk, Vicki, author.
Title: Growing up on the gridiron : football, friendship, and the tragic
    life of Owen Thomas / Vicki Mayk.
Description: Boston : Beacon Press, 2020. | Includes bibliographical
    references.
Identifiers: LCCN 2020011375 (print) | LCCN 2020011376 (ebook) |
    ISBN 9780807021927 (hardcover) | ISBN 9780807021965 (ebook)
Subjects: LCSH: Thomas, Owen, 1988-2010. | Chronic traumatic
    encephalopathy. | Football—Social aspects—United States. | Football
    players—Pennsylvania—Biography. | Allentown (Pa.)—Biography.
Classification: LCC GV939.T4445 M39 2020 (print) |
    LCC GV939.T4445 (ebook) | DDC 796.332092 [B]—dc23
LC record available at https://lccn.loc.gov/2020011375
LC ebook record available at https://lccn.loc.gov/2020011376

For my parents, Freda and Steve Jarmulowski,
with love and appreciation

CONTENTS

GROWING UP ON THE GRIDIRON

Owen Thomas after the University of Pennsylvania Quakers' victory against the Crimson of Harvard University on November 14, 2009, at Harvard Stadium. (Photo © Mickey Goldin)

APRIL 2010

THE BRAINS ARRIVE, usually by special courier, invariably packed in ice, to Dr. Ann McKee's lab at the VA-Boston University-Concussion Legacy Foundation Brain Bank. The containers in which they are shipped could be mistaken for the ones used to ship prime steaks. Brains, however, are softer than meat in the market. More delicate, more gelatinous. Researchers pressed for a description of a brain often liken it to the popular fruit-flavored dessert that jiggles.

McKee, director of Boston University's CTE Center and chief neuropathologist for the Brain Bank, never forgets that they belonged to human beings, people who lived, were loved, had hopes. Most of the brains delivered to her share something in common: they belonged to people who played sports in high school or college, or professionally. Most often, they belonged to men and boys who played football.

McKee speaks freely and informally to the people who visit her office and lab. She has a directness that probably can be traced back to her Midwestern roots growing up in Wisconsin. The directness is underscored when McKee makes eye contact with her bright blue eyes. Sometimes that gaze is muted by her oversized glasses. But when a visitor comes to her office at the VA, the glasses are likely to be sitting on her desk, somewhere amid the stacks of papers and the towers of stained slides. A white lab coat covers her shirt and slacks. She's one of the foremost researchers—*the* leading CTE researcher, the one most frequently associated with the disease. CTE, or chronic traumatic encephalopathy, is a progressive degenerative brain disease caused by repeated brain trauma. The trauma can be in the form of powerful blows to the head that cause concussions. It also can come from other jarring blows that cause the brain to rattle within the skull like an amusement park bumper car. Such blows are sustained by soldiers exposed to bomb blasts in combat and by football players, soccer players, hockey players, boxers. Researchers assessing traumatic brain injury in sports call this second category of trauma subconcussive hits. While such hits are not powerful enough to cause a full-blown concussion, in 2010 researchers began to realize that they were enough to do the damage that can lead to CTE.[1]

CTE is characterized by a buildup in the brain of a protein called tau. Brains are made up of 90 billion neurons, which relay signals through long fibers called axons. When the axons are jarred, they can break, releasing toxins. That's when a concussion occurs and with it often comes a host of symptoms: headaches, confusion, fatigue, blurred vision, problems with sleep and mood. Time and rest are required for the brain to recover.

Unlike the more obvious symptoms of concussions, which appear relatively quickly, CTE symptoms burgeon over time. Tau protein supports microtubules found in the axons, the brain's signal carriers mentioned earlier. When the microtubules come apart—because of concussions or repeated jarring blows to the head—the tau protein is dislodged and begins to clump together, breaking down communication between neurons. Eventually, brain degeneration results and the condition known as CTE can occur—causing memory loss, confusion, impaired judgment, impulse control problems, aggression, depression, and, for some, dementia. Once underway, tau buildup never stops. Insidiously, it continues to grow, even after an individual stops playing football or hockey or any other activity that may have caused the initial damage. The presence of CTE can be confirmed only after death, by researchers like Ann McKee.[2]

McKee's obsession with CTE can be traced to 2003, when she performed an autopsy on a seventy-two-year-old veteran who had been diagnosed with Alzheimer's disease fifteen years earlier. Under her microscope, she saw patterns of tau protein in a totally unfamiliar pattern. There was no evidence of the beta-amyloid plaques that are present in Alzheimer's patients. The veteran turned out to have been a boxer. Two years later, in 2005, the same strange pattern of tau showed up in another patient. A call to his family revealed he, too, had been a pugilist.[3]

McKee was recruited to head CTE research at Boston University in 2008, a year after Dr. Robert Cantu, a neurologist, neurosurgeon, and leading concussion expert, and activist Chris Nowinski, PhD, founded the Sports Legacy Institute and created the center's precursor, the Boston University Center for the Study of Traumatic Encephalopathy. The institute would later become the Sports Legacy Foundation, with a goal of raising awareness about the dangers of concussions, particularly among young athletes.[4]

No longer encased in a skull under a thatch of flaming red hair, a brain arrives at McKee's lab. McKee doesn't know about the red hair. What she does know is that this was the brain of a college football player. He was in his early twenties. He committed suicide. Any more details could prejudice her work, she says.

The brain belonged to Owen Thomas.

McKee's lab has detailed procedures for dealing with specimens. When Owen's brain arrives, it is weighed, photographed, and visually inspected for evidence of trauma or disease. It's then preserved with periodate-lysine-paraformaldehyde, referred to as PLP, a solution preferred by McKee and her colleagues because it keeps the brain tissue a bit softer than do other preservatives used in labs. Samples are taken from twenty-eight separate areas of the brain. The rest of the brain is frozen for future investigation, while the samples are sent to histology technicians, who dehydrate them and embed them in paraffin wax. The process makes them easier to slice. The technicians use a special tool called a microtome that slices extremely thin sections of tissue for study. How thin? Thinner than you can imagine. Twenty microns. That's the width of a human hair. The slices are mounted on slides, which are each stained from two to six times with antibodies that will reveal the target proteins that will confirm the presence of CTE.

It's late in the day when McKee turns her attention to Owen's case. The late afternoon sunlight has already ceded to evening. Twilight touches the Boston streets outside. She likes working after hours, when she's the only one in the lab. "A lot of times, you get into your zen of looking at the case," McKee says. "It's quiet; it's very meditative for me, as I'm looking through the case." That night, she expects she'll be able to hurry through. It should not take long with a subject this young.

In the silence of the lab, she looks at tissue from Owen Thomas's frontal cortex under the microscope. She is shocked at what she sees. "Repeatedly in his brain, over and over, I saw areas of abnormalities that I've never seen except in association with CTE," McKee says.

The buildup of tau protein she sees is everywhere, with twenty areas of Owen's brain affected—twenty areas where tau protein would continue to grow over time if Owen had lived. McKee and her colleagues assign different levels—called grades—to indicate the severity of the disease, with grade 1 the lowest level, with least incidence of disease, and 4 the highest. At just twenty-one, Owen Thomas already had grade 2 CTE, the most advanced level found to date for a football player at his age.

When McKee is done examining Owen's brain, she drives to her home in suburban Boston, deeply troubled. How could this be? How could someone so young commit suicide? How could someone so young have this degree of disease? She thinks of her own son, Graham, then almost the same age as Owen, and what his loss would mean. After arriving home that night, she's unable to sleep. She watches a documentary on HBO about a young man who commits suicide.

Ann McKee is haunted by Owen's case and by the loss of his young life. A decade later, she will continue to be haunted. She remembers Owen Thomas no matter how many other brains come under her microscope.

"That case, I'll never forget. That was life-changing," McKee says without hesitation. "There are certain cases and certain moments that really alter your perception of things. And that certainly was the case with Owen Thomas."

CHAPTER 1

GAME CHANGER

THE PARKLAND HIGH SCHOOL stadium in Orefield, Pennsylvania, tops a hill like a crown on the head of a king, its lights casting a glow that blocks the stars. The weather had turned colder by mid-November—not frigid, but pleasantly cool in the fifties. Perfect football weather, more than one person remarked as they ambled into the stadium. Some toted square plastic seat cushions to soften their perch on bleachers. A few brought blankets to guard against the evening's chill.

This is football on a Friday night in suburbia, played in a community where acres of farmland north and west of the city of Allentown, Pennsylvania, have slowly yielded to become acres of homes over the decades. Within the Parkland School District's seventy-two square miles, housing developments with names like Green Hills and Orchard View Estates recall the plowed fields that gave way to the houses. Among Parkland residents, the kind of house you live in becomes a kind of economic calling card. The kind of house you live in defines your socioeconomic group.

Parents giving their child's friend a ride home after the football game might size up the family's financial status as soon as they pull in the driveway. If the residence boasts a polished oak front door opening into a three-thousand-square-foot luxury home on a half-acre or acre lot, it's likely that it's owned by one of the doctors who practice medicine at Lehigh Valley Hospital, or by a lawyer, or maybe by a researcher at Air Products and Chemicals. An annual household income of six figures or more is indicated. If it's a more modest home—a split level, ranch, or maybe a twin home in a development like Schnecksville North—it's probably owned by someone with a more modest annual income. A teacher, perhaps, or someone moderately successful in sales. Maybe a professor at one of the area's half-dozen colleges and universities. Youngsters who are dropped off at their home in Lil Wolf or Green Acres—two large mobile home parks in the school district—or at an old house that has been divided into apartments clearly come from families with more modest means. The children who live in those houses also are more likely to be among the 27 percent of the district's 9,400 students eligible to receive a free lunch.[1] All of the children from all of these houses meet in Parkland School District's classrooms and on its athletic fields. The parents—whether traveling in a BMW SUV or a used Chevy—come together on nights like this for football. Success in football or other sports and academic achievement are the accomplishments most prized by a majority of Parkland's parents.

The crowd gathering at the stadium climbs onto the bleachers, the banter building to a hum of anticipation, reflecting that this is more than a routine game, more than just another contest under the Friday night lights. The Parkland High School Trojans are facing Easton High School's Red Rovers in the Pennsylvania Interscholastic Athletic Association District 11 finals. The game decides who moves on to compete in "states," the single-word shorthand for the state championship. The Trojans, coming off an undefeated season, have already bested East Stroudsburg's Cavaliers 21–7 in the first round of postseason play.[2] Such a season makes it easy to forget that Easton has a history in playoffs against Parkland, a three-game winning streak that in other years has crushed the Trojans' hopes of postseason glory.

The Trojans have every reason to think this year could be different. Their 2006 season included six shutouts against many of the Lehigh Valley's toughest and most respected teams. Parkland's offensive and defensive lines are filled with veteran players, many of them seniors who have been starters since they were freshmen. They include starting quarterback Marc Quilling and offensive tackle Mike Fay. For the rest of their lives, Quilling will remember Fay as more than a friend: throughout their high school years, Fay was the one protecting Quilling's blind side, keeping him from getting pummeled as he went out for a pass. It's the kind of relationship that makes playing high school football more than a game. It's a brotherhood with relationships as solid as those formed by soldiers in the trenches of war. In its own way, even on this amateur level, that is how this sport is viewed: as a battle, replete with terms like blitz and bomb to describe the play. It's no accident that this team is called the Trojans, honoring some of history's most storied warriors.

Head coach Jim Morgans, who has spent more than thirty years coaching high school football, has seen his share of winning teams. If you include his time playing the game before he became a coach, he's spent over forty years of his life focused on football. When he came to Parkland from coaching at his alma mater, Allentown Central Catholic High School, two years earlier, he realized that he had an exceptional group of players. Yes, many were talented athletes, but Morgans saw their success as a result of other attributes.

"They were a very tight-knit group, a very tight-knit team," Morgans says. "They understood the meaning of team. Their personal goals were put behind team goals."

He explains that a commitment to team goals includes a willingness to commit hours to grueling practices and a strength and conditioning program that requires players to lift weights before school starts at 8 a.m. It means that no player is focused on his own accomplishments to the detriment of his teammates. Morgans has no doubt that this shared commitment has brought his team success, that it's helped bring them to this playoff on a Friday night in November 2006.

|||||||||||||

The stadium is filled with the cacophony of warring marching bands playing fight songs, cheerleaders chanting, the crowd cheering. A few fans have already paid an early visit to the refreshment stand, manned by the Parkland Football Booster Club and parents of marching band members. Anyone nearing the stand, separated from the end zone by a running track, is drawn by the irresistible mingled scents of popcorn, grilling hot dogs, and coffee. A sudden fanfare draws the attention of everyone to the field.

Parkland's team enters the stadium in their gray and red uniforms, breaking through an oversized paper banner, big as a bedsheet, held by members of the cheerleading squad. It's emblazoned with messages urging them to victory: "Go Trojans," "Wreck the Red Rovers," "Make it 12–0."

Moments after the kickoff, it is clear that things are going wrong for the Trojans. The Red Rovers are outplaying them, shutting down their defense and blocking their scoring attempts, play after play. As halftime approaches, the crowd on the Parkland side of the field has grown quiet, eyeing the scoreboard in disbelief. The undefeated Parkland Trojans are down 14–0. On the bench, players are visibly shaken.

But for one of them, defeat can only come after a fight.

On a fourth-down play, as the Red Rovers are driving to score, one of their receivers breaks free. Suddenly, he is taken out by a bone-crunching hit that seems to come out of nowhere. The tackler, wisps of his shoulder-length red hair visible around the edges of his silver-gray helmet, has the look of a Viking. And that's how number 31, Trojan team captain Owen Thomas, sees himself. He is a warrior, prepared to fight to the last. No surprise for an eighteen-year-old who counts the film

300 among his favorites. It recounts the story of the badly out-numbered Spartan soldiers who fought to the last man at the Battle of Thermopylae in the Persian War.

Back on his feet after the tackle, Owen turns toward his teammates, fists clenched, and roars an exhortation.

"Let's fucking go!"

The playoffs are especially important to Owen. Making it to the postseason is part of his family's football tradition. Owen's older brother Morgan, an offensive lineman, had played on Parkland's 2002 state championship team on his way to earning a place in the school district's athletic hall of fame. Earlier, his brother Matt, who set a statewide rushing record in 1996, was on a Parkland team that won the District XI title to make it to the PIAA semifinal before buckling.[3] Now it was Owen's turn.

"That hit, you could probably feel it all the way up to the top of the stands," Trojan offensive lineman Jamie Pagliaro recalls. Pags, as he's known to his teammates, has a reputation for remembering plays from key games down to the last detail. He will always remember this one. "It was one of the biggest hits I've ever seen in my life. After that, we just kicked it into second gear."

Parkland scores on the next drive and never gives up another point for the remainder of the game. In the fourth quarter, they are ahead 15–14. Then comes a play that Marc Quilling would remember in agonizing slow motion as he replayed it in memory. Faking a pass before throwing to Pags, Marc does not see a linebacker coming from the back who smacks down the ball. The Red Rovers regain possession, but they are unable to score. Then a referee calls a penalty on a Trojan player for roughing the passer. What is normally a fifteen-yard penalty is measured incorrectly, giving the Red Rovers additional yardage. The error puts the Easton team into easy field-goal position, allowing them to hand Parkland a crushing defeat as they win 17–15. Coach Morgans later receives a letter of apology from the PIAA about the officiating mistake that he is sure led to the loss.

Coach Morgans resented the loss, not for himself, but for the members of his team—particularly those ending their high school playing careers. The loss also marked the end of their football careers. Only 7.1 percent of high school players go on to play in college.[4]

"I'm going to continue to coach, but there's fifty kids, fifty-five, who are never going to play football anymore. They're done. They're done with high school football. Not that many kids go on," Morgans says.

||||||||||||

Everyone on the team would remember the loss. They would also remember Owen's game-changing tackle. Hard hits are the stuff of American football legend, from high school games through the pros. New York Giants football great Y. A. Tittle bleeding as he sits on the sidelines in a 1964 game against the Pittsburgh Steelers is one of the most iconic sports photos of all time.[5] New York Giants linebacker Lawrence Taylor breaking Washington Redskins quarterback Joe Theismann's leg, ending Theismann's career, is recalled by fans decades later.[6] But no one speculates about what those hits cost them in the long run—just as no one speculated about what leveling the Easton player might have cost Owen. Considering what is now known about the effects of subconcussive hits on players' brains, it's reasonable to surmise that Owen's memorable tackle in the regional championship may have exacted a price. It was yet another hard hit in a decade of them that started when he began playing football at age nine. The price would be apparent later.

But in 2006, despite the heartbreak of the playoff loss, Owen had assured his place in Parkland football history: a player and team captain who was tough, physical, and inspiring. To a man, his teammates and coaches would say, "Owen was a born football player."

CHAPTER 2

BIRTH OF A VIKING

OWEN THOMAS CAME into the world screaming.

His face matched his flaming red hair and the veins on both sides of his neck stood out.

"A Viking," the doctor pronounced examining the newborn.

Tom Thomas, assisting at the birth on September 30, 1988, was doing double duty. Nurses were scarce that day in Allentown's Sacred Heart Hospital, so he kept an eye on the contraction monitor while serving as labor coach to his wife, Kathy Brearley. He remembers his youngest son's first sound.

"It was a passionate, intense scream, as if he were saying, 'Here I am. I'm in the world,'" Tom Thomas says. "It was that intensity he always had." They named him Owen, a Celtic name meaning young fighter.

Years later, the intensity became his trademark on the playing field, an innate drive that made opponents wary of his ferocious hits. But that day, as his mother looked down at her son's eyes—the same vivid blue as her own—she only worried how he'd fit into a busy household with three older brothers. His birth completed a family that had begun when she first met Tom on the other side of the world.

Tom and Kathy met while serving as teachers and missionaries in Zambia. A graduate of Andover Newton Theological Seminary in Massachusetts, Tom was already an ordained minister when he arrived. His journey to Africa was preceded by assignments at churches in Linsport, Kansas, and Portland, Maine. Both were formative experiences for the young minister.

When he arrived in Kansas for a one-year ministerial internship, he found himself in a farming community dubbed Little Sweden because of its strong ethnic roots. Members of the congregation had just finished cleaning the enormous seven-bedroom parsonage that rose like a monument on the flat prairie. As they were leaving, the car carrying their new pastor pulled up. Out stepped someone who looked like one of the Vietnam War protestors of the era. Coming from Boston, Tom sported long reddish-brown hair and an equally long beard. There was a moment of silence before introductions began.

"The men had on their John Deere hats. . . . Everybody was farm-related. How could we respond to each other?" Tom says, remembering both sides had cautiously assessed each other on their first meeting. "But by the end of the year, I knew. You talk about the price of wheat. You talk about the rainfall. You talk about what they're interested in. It was a great year, but I had to adapt to that culture. They weren't going to adapt to me. I made friends with some of the most conservative members of the congregation, because I shoveled out their manure."

The lesson had a permanent impact. Over the years, people would often remark on Tom's ability to empathize and interact with all kinds of people. It was something he'd pass on to his sons.

After returning to seminary to complete his training, Tom was sent to State Street Church in Portland, Maine, after his ordination. The four-year assignment was not as affirming as his Kansas sojourn. He served as associate pastor. When the senior pastor retired, the new pastor made it clear he wanted no associate. It was the second ending for Tom while living in Maine. An early marriage to his high school sweetheart also had ended while he was there. It left him free to fulfill a long-time dream of serving in Latin America or Africa.

"I was always interested in liberation movements and changing civilizations," Tom says. The change also meant he was single when he met Kathy Brearley.

Tom worked at the United Church of Zambia's Kafue Secondary School while Kathy taught at Chipembe, a neighboring girls school. Zambia's capital city, Lusaka, separated the two institutions. Kathy, who had a degree in math, had worked as a systems engineer for British Aerospace when she responded to a call for people who could teach math in Africa. She arrived in Zambia in January 1979. Tom received his assignment via the United Church of Christ and arrived in September of that year.

"The first time I saw him, he was digging his vegetable garden without his shirt on. I can't say that impressed me too much," Kathy says with characteristic bluntness. "Later that day or the next day, it must have been a school holiday, he and some friends were out on a grassy soccer field playing Frisbee.

"I am the most uncoordinated person. . . . Tom was so graceful. Someone would throw to him and he'd just put out his arm like this," she adds, chuckling as she pantomimes the long, fluid motion of her future husband's arm.

She soon learned that Tom had played football in college at the University of Virginia. Having grown up in Great Britain, she had little understanding what it meant to play football in the States. She only knew that it was different than rugby, which was her home country's version of the sport. When they began dating, she would learn that his athleticism made it hard for her to keep up on long bike rides.

Tom drove the school truck that also functioned as a bus to shuttle male students back and forth for joint activities at the girls school or to take Sunday school teachers there for combined training. One trip provided an unusual chapter in their early relationship.

"I got malaria when I was at Kathy's school and I couldn't drive back, so I stayed in Kathy's house," he says, a bemused smile crossing his face. It was unheard of to allow two unmarried people of the opposite sex to stay in the same house, but the severity of Tom's illness was insurance against impropriety.

"His temperature was 105; he was delirious," Kathy says. "He kept babbling on about Richard Nixon."

After Tom recovered, romance eventually blossomed. They became engaged in April 1980 and married in August. Tom's parents visited at the time of their engagement, while Kathy's parents and sister came to Zambia for the wedding.

Kathy went to the market in Lusaka and bought hand-printed Zambian fabric to make her wedding dress and a shirt for Tom. Held after Sunday services, the ceremony and celebration were well attended. "Since I was a pastor, people came from all over from all of the parishes I served. And the reception was in our yard," Tom recalls. He wore a black shirt with patterns in red, beige, and white. A pineapple-shaped motif extended from the open neck of the shirt to its midsection. Kathy's empire-waist gown's bodice was in the same bright fabric as her groom's shirt, topping a long white skirt. She wore a head wreath of red blossoms and carried a large bouquet of native flowers, so informally arranged that they could have been plucked from the ground that morning. The young couple exited the church, Kathy on Tom's arm, and walked into the blinding African sunlight. The menu at the reception included chicken, rice, a kale-like vegetable called rape, and crates of Coca-Cola to wash it down—served without ice. The wedding party sat at a long table under a small tree that cast what passed for shade in the hot climate.

Their most memorable wedding present was a hen—given so that a young couple would not have to waste time going out for food. They would be free to spend their time in conjugal relations while the hen supplied eggs. Because the hen was redheaded, they named her after Kathy's mother, Hazel, who had the flaming hair that Owen would inherit. "She was always frowning and always running backwards and forwards looking for something," Kathy says. "Which is what my mother did and what I do now. So we called her Hazel."

The couple returned to the States in 1982, settling in Lancaster, Pennsylvania, where Kathy began studying for the ministry at Lancaster Theological Seminary. When Tom was called to be pastor of Union United Church of Christ in 1984, they moved to Neffs, a suburb twelve miles north of the city of Allentown in Pennsylvania's Lehigh Valley. The redbrick church's beautiful steeple, visible for miles over the surrounding countryside, dates back to the 1800s when Pennsylvania Germans built it in their farming community. The couple settled into the parsonage, an updated Cape Cod a short distance from the church. Fronting busy Route 873, the house was a place where they could start their family as Tom began his ministry.

The Brearley-Thomas household grew rapidly. "We went from two to a family of six in three years' time," Tom recalls. The couple became foster parents to two brothers, Jerry and Matt, then seven and five. In 1987, Kathy delivered their son Morgan, and shortly after, their adoption of Jerry and Matt was finalized. "I remember holding Morgan when I was testifying in Reading [Pennsylvania] for the adoption process," Tom says. By the next year, Kathy was pregnant again with Owen.

She had worried how her youngest son would fit into the household. "I thought, 'If we don't create a space for him to be himself, he's not going to be able have his own identity.' But we never had to worry about that." She pauses and her tone turns rueful. "Not once did we have to worry about that, about Owen having space to be himself. Owen created plenty of space to be himself. He came with this incredible energy and this very strong opinion of who he was and what he wanted."

Being able to hold his own was an asset in a house where relationships among his older siblings were frequently in turmoil. The adopted boys—children of a mother who struggled with addiction—brought myriad problems. "Jerry and Matt were just always at each other. Or there was always conflict or tension all the time. It really was often very unpleasant being with them," Tom recalls. "They were always squabbling and fighting. And this wasn't normal brother stuff. This was more serious. Matt still will have no relationship with Jerry. He just hates Jerry so much."

The situation became overwhelming. Jerry, who suffered from severe mental illness, was placed in institutional care at the end of fifth grade when Owen was a toddler. His complicated diagnosis, involving several conditions, required a combination of medication. Tom says the volatile nature of the older boys' relationship affected the parenting of the younger two. "Kathy and I both realize now we didn't have the time to spend with Morgan and Owen because we also had Jerry and Matt. And they demanded so much attention," Tom says.

The younger boys had their own dynamic. Morgan displayed a laid-back demeanor. Owen, younger by a bit more than a year, approached every situation with a desire to be first. "There was a television show around that time, *Charles in Charge*, and his goal in life was to be the boss in charge," Tom says. "That was his phrase, 'The boss in charge.'"

A trip to the park when Owen was three and Morgan just over four reflected their personalities. When their mother suggested that they could pretend to be an army and march behind a commander, Owen announced, "I'll have to be the commander."

"Now, with our older boys, Matt and Jerry, who were also close in age, that would be an endless fight; we'd have to get in the car and go home. Morgan just happily said, 'I'll be last.' Morgan wants people to be happy and for everyone to have a good time," their mother says.

Owen's intensity juxtaposed against Morgan's happy-go-lucky nature played out in many aspects of their lives. When Morgan visited the doctor for earaches or other childhood illnesses, he sat placidly through the examination. Owen screamed from the moment the doctor entered the room. His father recalls being asked to help hold him down during treatment.

The biological brothers differed in stature as well as personality. Morgan's size placed him among children two or more years his senior in sports and other activities. Owen was clearly the little brother. "He was a scrawny kid," says the Reverend Kris Snyder-Samuelson, the youth minister and Tom's associate pastor at Union United Church of Christ. "You never thought he'd be a football player."

The rough and tumble life that comes with being the youngest of four boys wasn't without mishaps for Owen. "I gave him a bunch of stitches," Morgan says, his eyes twinkling in his round face. Once, as the boys were running around the first floor of the church parsonage, Owen fell and hit his head on a radiator. Another time Morgan pushed Owen, causing him to hit his head on a wooden sofa frame. An argument over who could play with their father's golf clubs ended with Morgan whacking Owen over the head with one of the clubs. If their hijinks didn't involve physical injury, it sometimes led to property damage. Owen shot out a neighbor's windows with a BB gun. On another occasion, a passing car's headlight was damaged as the boys bounced a ball across the street in traffic while waiting for the school bus.

"Sometimes I feel bad for my dad and my mom for how mischievous we were," Morgan says.

The pair never squelched their behavior—even in their father's church. Sofas in a church conference room became trampolines, with the boys doing elbow drops. In the children's choir, Owen was the loudest and the most energetic. On one memorable Sunday, while adults sipped coffee during the social hour in the church hall after services, Owen and his buddies returned to the sanctuary, dove headfirst under the first pew and made their wriggling way under the long rows of white pews, commando style, to the back.

Impish, fearless behavior characterized his childhood. "He was just always exuberant. Anything he did, he was exuberant,"

Tom adds. "Once he was jumping on a picnic table. And he danced right off the end of it. And I was there to catch him." Tom's voice cracks as he recalls the moment, several years after his son's death. He composes himself, reflecting. "He was never intimidated. I never remember him being intimidated."

|||||||||||||

Owen may have inherited his love of aggressive play on the gridiron from his paternal grandfather. Frank R. Thomas played in the 1930s as one of J. P. McCaskey High School's Red Tornados. The Lancaster, Pennsylvania, school was one where "they took their football seriously," Owen's father recalls, and it matched Frank Thomas's dedication to the sport. When it came time for college, he attended nearby Millersville State Teachers College so he could live at home to help his widowed mother. He still found time to be a running back for the Millersville Marauders.

A passion for the physicality of the game was a trait that Owen shared with his grandfather. "My father always loved football. Even in his sixties, he'd be watching football and say, 'Ah, I'd like to get in there and tackle someone,'" Tom says.

Football was a different game in the 1930s and 1940s when Frank Thomas played. In those days, it was still more of a ground game, compared to the aerial passing game known today, with the forward pass just beginning to gain traction. Helmets were not mandatory until 1943, and the players who did wear them were probably wearing leather helmets, because the first plastic helmet was not introduced until 1939.[1] Shoulder pads during the era when the elder Thomas played were leather and offered less protection than the pads worn today.[2] Even the football itself did not evolve to the standard size and shape that is now found on playing fields until 1935.[3] In that bygone era, many men played both offense and defense. But perhaps the most important difference was in the size of the players. Frank Thomas weighed around 160 pounds when he played as a running back and was considered a good size. Players were considered really big at 200 pounds. Over the decades, the average weight of lineman increased, topping 300 pounds in the last two decades. And with their increase in size have come more powerful hits, blocks, and tackles.[4] The era of bigger, stronger, faster players was the era in which Owen and his brothers took the field.

The Thomases are typical of many American families. Football is a tradition—a sports legacy passed down through generations. Family dynasties in the sport exist from high school teams all the way up through college and the pros. In the NFL, families like the Mannings—father, Archie, and sons Peyton and Eli, who all had long careers as pro quarterbacks—are the stuff of legend. For every high-profile family dynasty of players, there are thousands more on the amateur level.

Fathers encourage sons to play football as a rite of passage that instills discipline and teaches lessons of bravery and loyalty. Others may encourage their sons to go out for the team so that their offspring can fulfill the dreams of gridiron glory that eluded them. For others, it means continuing the history of family success on the field. Owen's grandfather, father, and two older brothers were gridiron standouts. It was natural that he would become a third-generation football player.

The legacy of the Thomases on the football field might have ended with Frank Thomas if his son Tom had a choice. Big and solidly built, Tom fit the physical profile of a football player even as a boy. There was no team in the Lampeter-Strasburg School District in rural Lancaster County where Tom entered junior high. Realizing his son's size would be an asset, Frank hauled him to tryouts for the all-Lancaster team, a squad that played all over the county. "I didn't want to do it. I just remember that my father put me in the car and I remember being so scared," Tom says. Even then he was soft-spoken and displayed the gentle nature and low-key demeanor that his congregation would come to know well when he entered the ministry.

Despite his reservations, he made the team, playing both offense and defense on a squad that would be undefeated.

The senior Thomas's civil service career required a family move to Richmond, Virginia. Once there, Tom easily continued playing football. Entering a new junior-senior high school, he found being from Pennsylvania was an asset. "In those years, if you had played football in Pennsylvania, you were a star," he says, noting that long-standing winning traditions in a number of his home state's high schools created a halo effect for all who had played in the Keystone State. Pennsylvania's coal regions in the east and steel towns in the western part of the state produced legendary players such as Johnny Unitas, Joe Namath, and Joe Montana. Tom played fullback on offense and linebacker and defensive end on defense in Virginia. "Which, oddly enough, were the same positions Owen played," he muses.

He was good enough to snag a football scholarship to the University of Virginia, entering college in 1968 as an anthropology and sociology major. As a sophomore starting in the Cavaliers' season opener against Army, Tom was playing as a receiver on the kickoff and took a hit "that rang my bell," he said, employing the descriptor used by players for decades to describe a hit to the head. Shortly after, playing fullback on offense, he experienced a second head hit. Recalling his coach's admonition to try to walk off the field if injured, he did so—going right through the bewildered players in the Army defensive huddle as he headed for the sideline. "I can still see their faces. They looked at me like, 'What is this guy doing?'"

He received a medical redshirt for the remainder of the season because of the concussion. But Tom was not done with injuries. Playing on the practice squad after recovering, he was on his way to the ground after a tackle when a showboating defensive player hit him a second time, knocking off his helmet. "I didn't have a concussion, but I had double vision." He was assured by the athletic trainer that all he needed to do was ice the injury. When the double vision persisted for nearly a week,

Tom finally headed to the student health center. Referred to a specialist, he learned the hit had broken his orbit, the bony cavity that holds the muscles that attach the eye in the head. Surgery was needed to repair it.

Tom endured one more football injury during college: a separated shoulder. He does not look back on his playing career with particular fondness. The injuries alone would dissuade some, but Tom also felt separate from his teammates spiritually and philosophically. Already considering a career in the ministry, he could not relate to the newly formed Fellowship of Christian Athletes on the Virginia campus. The fellowship, a nondenominational Christian sports ministry, says in its vision statement that it aims to "see the world transformed by Jesus Christ through the influence of coaches and athletes."[5] "I couldn't understand what these people were saying—that a drop of sweat on the practice field is like a prayer to God," Tom says. He often felt alone.

"I probably was—and still am—different than the rest of the team. There wasn't a teammate that I found who was like a real colleague, someone I could share things with," Tom recalls. He found playing football in college had other drawbacks, ones that Owen and his teammates would experience years later. One of the most challenging was the fact that playing collegiate football left little time for anything else.

"Even then, it was a grind," Tom says, recalling the workouts, practices, and team meetings. "And it's much worse today than it was then. Then, we were all students first. Next to me was a mechanical engineer. Another person majored in chemistry. Football wasn't our life."

Talking to Tom about his football career, you get the impression the tradition of Thomases on the field could well have ended with him. His ambivalence about playing led him to encourage his sons to try other options. Unlike his father, who was determined that his son would play the sport he loved, Tom and his wife encouraged their boys to try other sports and activities. "I would have been happy if they had been doing band or doing something else," he says. "We certainly didn't live through their success." How football became central in the lives of three of his sons was more happenstance than the result of any encouragement from Tom.

Playing sports started early for the Thomas boys—but never early enough for Owen. When Morgan started playing T-ball, where the youngest players are introduced to baseball, Owen was still too young. "Owen appointed himself bat boy. He'd line the bats up, and told people when to get up. Owen found a role, took it, and acted the whole thing out. He was so confident," his mother Kathy says.

It was the same when Morgan entered an under-six soccer program. The team wore purple shirts and Kathy bought a similar one for Owen and made a logo so that he would feel like he was part of the team. Finally, searching for something that Owen could participate in before he was old enough for baseball and soccer, his mother enrolled him in a youth wrestling program. Even at four, he was ferocious in competition. "The coach would complain to us, 'Owen is so brutal in practice,'" his father says. Later, when Tom coached Morgan and Owen on an under-eight soccer team, it was his toughest year coaching.

Morgan remembers, "After one game, a coach or a parent from another team came up to my dad and said, 'Your son is so aggressive. This is soccer, this isn't football, and your son was doing this and doing that.' The thing was, this kid was two years older than Owen and Owen was bullying this kid on the soccer field."

As Owen entered elementary school, the year fell into a pattern marked not by academic milestones or holidays, but by sports seasons. At first it was baseball, soccer, and basketball. Jamie Pagliaro attended school with Owen from kindergarten through high school and played baseball, basketball, and football with him. The boys' involvement with organized sports was typical for kids in the United States. Youth sports is big business, growing in value annually over the last two decades to a high of over $19 billion, according to WinterGreen Research, which conducts market research about youth sports. The numbers of young people playing organized sports are equally large, with 4 million soccer players and 7.6 million tackle football players.[6]

Even in baseball, Owen dominated. As catcher, he blocked runners coming into home plate. "He defied this person to run into him," his mother, Kathy, says. The boys played on a baseball team dubbed "the Squirmies." "Everybody else in Schnecksville had the regular *S* on their hat, but ours was like squiggly, so we called ourselves the Squirmies," Jamie recalls. "And that year we went 20–0 in baseball and we won the championship. We were in fifth grade. My dad was one of the coaches. That was one of my big memories."

Owen was responsible for the championship game win, making a big play to throw someone out. "He was that guy I knew who would always give 110-percent effort. He was the guy I knew who would always change the game," Jamie says.

A friend presented Owen with a jar filled with dirt from the field. It was a memento that a Squirmies teammate claimed after his death.

| | | | | | | | | | | |

It was the Thomases' adoptive son Matt who made football the center of their lives. Starting as a soccer player while in middle school, Matt quickly became good enough to play on his community's first traveling team—an honor that soon proved a hardship for his parents who were juggling jobs, household responsibilities, and child rearing. Traveling teams—which have become a highly desirable level of play for many serious youth athletes—require significant investments of time and money for young players and their families. They offer the chance to play more competitive teams in other towns and even in other states. Many parents, convinced that their child's future success is tied to playing on such teams, spend thousands in a single season paying for gas, food, and hotels. If there is more than one child in the family, costs multiply. Some families willingly go into debt for the privilege of having their children play on a traveling team.[7] Ministerial salaries are relatively modest, but costs weren't the only consideration for Tom and Kathy. Weekends, when traveling teams play their games, are peak work times for clergy. Saturdays are spent preparing for services the next day—and sometimes include presiding at a wedding ceremony. On Sunday, the ministers officiated at two services at their respective churches. The needs of Matt's young siblings also were a factor.

"The teams were traveling to Maryland, to Ocean City, New Jersey, and we had two younger boys. So we said to Matt, 'Take a year off soccer. You can play any other sport, but take a year off soccer. Because we can't do this anymore.' And that's when he started playing football," Tom says.

It would be a decision that would affect the rest of their lives.

At first Matt hated the game, but it wasn't long before he became a star running back—one who set records at Parkland High School that stood until another star player, Austin Scott, broke them in 2003. Scott graduated from Parkland and went on to a short-lived Division I college career at Penn State. Matt, a gifted player at five feet, eight inches and 180 pounds, set season records for 2,322 yards rushing as a high school junior and twenty-three touchdowns as a senior. Also a good student, he was named scholar-athlete of the year in his senior year by the Lehigh Valley chapter of the National Football Foundation and College Hall of Fame.[8] He set a standard for his siblings—especially for Owen. "That became a magnet for Morgan and Owen," Tom says.

Owen would hang out with the older boys, easily holding his own, despite being the youngest. Matt and his friends invented a game called "Pop the Tart" in which Owen was tossed high in the air by the older boys, as if he were a Pop-Tart springing out of a toaster. He loved the roughhousing, returning again and again to be pummeled and tossed. In between, he trotted around the group carrying a football, mimicking the moves he had seen them make on the field.

The Thomas boys were among those who ensured football's position as the most popular sport in high schools in the United States. In 1996, when Matt and his Trojan teammates won the championship, 958,247 young men played high school football. When Owen donned pads to play for the first time a year later, the number had grown, with 972,114 playing for their high schools.[9]

Despite Matt's success and the irresistible attraction of the sport itself, Tom and Kathy kept the younger boys from playing football as long as they could. They succeeded in keeping Morgan from playing the contact sport until he was in seventh grade. In his case, the fact that he was big for his age actually kept him off the field. Teams in youth football are organized by weight to ensure that boys who are much bigger than others their age aren't grouped with smaller youth. The weight classification is a nod toward player safety, a concession that started long before concerns about concussions and head trauma. Morgan's size would have placed him with boys two years his senior if he had started playing on the peewee level. The Thomases felt it was better to wait.

CHAPTER 3

SUITING UP

BEHIND THE NONDESCRIPT white building that houses the Tri-Clover Fire Company on Kernsville Road, two back-to-back baseball fields sit like twin green thumbprints. A gray metal pole building boasts a sign for the North Parkland Athletic Association, the words printed over a silhouette of a buffalo. "Players and coaches only," announces a sign on the building's door—an attempt to deter overzealous parents from following their sons and daughters or arguing with coaches. The association, a volunteer-run organization, provides opportunities for boys and girls to get involved in sports—baseball, soccer, football, and cheerleading. Overly invested parents of young players are commonplace in youth sports, hounding coaches, screaming at referees, and shouting directions to players. The sign on the North Parkland building guarantees a space where players and coaches can communicate without parental interference.

The fields behind the fire company are home base for some of the association's teams, and they do double duty. When baseball season is over, they yield a large, grassy area big enough for young football players to run drills. Parents can watch from beat-up bleachers ringing the field while the boys practice tackling, passing, and blocking. As the fall weather turns cooler, the boys' breath hangs like clouds in the air as the shrill sounds of coaches' whistles punctuate the drills.

This is where Owen and his teammates began their football careers. Owen—with characteristic determination—convinced his parents to allow him to start playing in North Parkland's youth football league when he was nine and entering fourth grade. He joined a team for players in the ninety-pound weight group.

At the first practice, Owen burst from the car, impatient to begin. While volunteer coaches called the roll and organized their young players into groups for calisthenics and drills, he bounced from foot to foot. Every time his feet hit the dirt, they seemed to pound out a rhythm that said "Football. Football. Football. Football." His energy stood out. Most of the young players were enthusiastic. A few were fearful, warily sizing up the other boys who would eventually be tackling them. Owen was ecstatic.

Marc Quilling was there from the beginning.

IIIIIIIIIIII

"I was from Kernsville [School] and he was from Schnecks-ville," Marc says. "I'll always remember him as being overly excited to play football. He was this outgoing, personable kid who approached everyone with a smile."

Marc had been playing football for several years before Owen became a teammate. He began playing flag football—the lowest level of play, which involves no tackling—at age five. Like Owen, Marc's interest in the sport was spawned by watching his older brother, Ryan, two years his senior, play first. And like the Thomas family, the Quilling boys also followed in their father's footsteps when they stepped onto the gridiron. In his home state of Ohio, Marc's father, Scott, was a multisport athlete who played football for two years as a walk-on punter at Ohio State University under legendary coach Woody Hayes. Earlier, Marc's great uncle had been a running back for the Buckeyes on one of Hayes's teams. Yet Marc insists there was never any pressure from his father to play. "He got us involved in it because both my brother and I were so interested in it from a young age," Marc says. "It's almost in our blood, you know?"

If it was not in their blood, it was certainly part of their psyche. In addition to watching brothers play and hearing the intoxicating tales of fathers, uncles, and grandfathers suiting up, the boys were immersed in a culture in which football plays a central role. By the late 1990s, football clearly was an obsession for many in the United States, whether as a fan or a player. It was the decade that spawned one of the most highly praised books about the sport, *Friday Night Lights: A Town, a Team, and a Dream*, H. G. Bissinger's nonfiction account of a high school football team in Odessa, Texas. Although the book reflected the racial divide and social strain, it also captured the drama in a town where football was king. Readers identified with the players whose stories are told in the book.

Football's popularity started long before. Since the earliest days of football, in the late 1800s—when the sport was introduced in America on the collegiate level—America's interest in the game has grown exponentially over the decades. With the introduction of radio and later television to broadcast games, football came to occupy a singular part of America's consciousness.[1] It is a sport with loyalty built via the media, and its ascendance in popularity is tied to how well it plays on television. The start of the professional sport as we know it in the United States is often acknowledged to be the broadcast of the 1958 championship game between the Baltimore Colts and New York Giants. Dubbed "The Greatest Game Ever Played," the contest went into sudden-death overtime while a large TV audience watched.[2] Games once broadcast only on weekends became a popular prime-time staple with the introduction of *Monday Night Football* in 1970. Games would be broadcast on other nights of the week as decades passed. By the time Owen and his friends began playing football, the Super Bowl had set records as one of the most-watched television shows each year—and would remain such in the years to come, when as much as a third of the viewing population in the United States tuned in. Games were true stories filled with gallant warriors who risked everything for victory—an enticing tale that invited young athletes to become part of the narrative. Little wonder that interest exists in boys as young as five.

Jamie Pagliaro already had been Owen's teammate on the Squirmies baseball team and on the basketball court. He was happy to finally see his friend on the football field. Like Marc, Jamie had been playing youth football for several seasons before Owen started. Although he enjoyed playing multiple sports, Jamie had a clear preference, even in elementary school. "Football was always number one," he says. He, too, claimed the sport as his birthright—although in his case, the affinity was inherited from his mother's side of the family. His maternal grandfather, Joe Beblavy, had played for Kutztown University of Pennsylvania—then Kutztown State—as tight end, defensive end, and kicker—the latter a position that earned him the nickname "Joe the Toe." Later Beblavy coached at Allentown's Trexler Middle School. The coaching would extend to his grandson. "Football was everything," Jamie says.

When the boys donned pads and uniforms, it was easy to imagine Marc as the quarterback. Even in elementary school, he already displayed the boyish handsomeness associated with the stereotype of the team's star player. Owen, thin and impish looking under his flaming red hair, had yet to grow into the formidable physical presence on the field that he would become by high school. He seemed nearly dwarfed by his pads. Jamie, despite his propensity for fierce play, had a round, almost baby-like face under his helmet.

Marc, Jamie, and Owen played for the North Parkland Athletic Association Buffaloes—named, no doubt, for the animals grazing placidly at the nearby Trexler Game Preserve. From their first season, Owen and Marc played the positions they would fill on football teams through high school and college. Marc played quarterback. In youth football, Jamie played tight end and backup quarterback. Owen almost naturally gravitated to defensive positions, playing linebacker and safety early on. "I just remember Owen being ready to hit someone from that first time he got a helmet on. That's what he wanted," Marc says.

It was something he had in common with Jamie. "I just liked hitting people," Jamie says.

Not all young players come to the game ready to tackle or be tackled. Coaches working with new football players, regardless of the players' ages, always needed to help boys overcome their fear of contact. In the age of the internet, articles with titles like "Overcoming Natural Fear of Contact" offered coaches tips to help their players become comfortable with the hits that define tackle football.[3] Today, alternative ways of tackling, such as shoulder tackling, aim to minimize head injury, and training programs are offered to teach coaches how to implement them.[4] Those alternatives weren't practiced in 1997 when Owen and his teammates started playing the game.

Owen didn't need to overcome any reticence. He arrived ready to tackle and be tackled. Family and teammates remember his fearless play from an early age. The sound of helmets cracking punctuated practice.

Despite the intensity of Owen's play, it was Marc who was injured that first season. A teammate's helmet caught his right hand—the one he used for throwing the football as quarterback—and by the end of the quarter, it had swelled to twice its size. Marc showed it to his coach, who squinted at it briefly, and declared, "Oh, you're OK. Go back down there." Marc finished practice, but he ended up with a broken hand that required a cast for more than six weeks. In addition to ending the football season, it cheated him out of the last weeks at the community pool at Neffs Valley Park.

For most kids in North Parkland, the pool at Neffs was the center of summer activity. Tucked in a wooded area off of the Neffs Laurys Road, it was one of two pools providing relief from the summer heat. The Orchard View Swim Club, a private club, was favored by more affluent families. Orchard View families had to buy bonds to secure their places in the swim club, as well as pay annual dues. A high wooden fence assured their privacy. Neffs Valley Park was the community pool where anyone could swim by paying a one-time admission or buying a season pass for a modest fee. A chain-link fence surrounded the huge pool, and a locker room as well as a slightly dilapidated snack bar selling ice cream, candy, and bad pizza dominated one end. By late summer, the boys divided their time between football practices and hanging out at the pool. To lose time both at the pool and playing football was double punishment, but Marc took it with the easygoing attitude that he would display into adulthood, a smile always ready.

His loss at quarterback also contributed to the Buffaloes losing the championship to their rivals from the South Parkland Athletic Association. The counterpart to the North Parkland league, it provided youth sports opportunities in the southern part of the sprawling Parkland School District. The sense of rivalry between North Parkland and South Parkland was shared by players and their parents, creating a kind of suburban civil war with victors claiming bragging rights.

Mike Fay was one of those South Parkland rivals. But unlike Owen and Marc, he had not come willingly to the gridiron. A big kid who was overweight in elementary school, he often felt alone and isolated. He looked in the mirror, fixating on his ears that seemed big and floppy in the self-conscious assessment of a preadolescent. His father had bought him a pass to the Allentown Municipal Golf Course, and he spent hours golfing, strolling the greens, and feeling more at home there than he did anywhere else.

"I just want to be a golfer," Mike told his father when the question of playing a sport came up.

"No, you're going to play football," his father told him.

"But what about what I want?" Mike asked.

"You can do what you want when you're eighteen," was the rejoinder.

Although his father had never played, his two brothers, Joey and Anthony, nine and seven years older, respectively, had both been successful for Parkland as defensive backs. It was a daunting legacy for the youngest brother. Anthony set records at the high school for interceptions and punt returns. Joey went on to play for the US Naval Academy, while Anthony played for two years at the University of Pennsylvania before a career-ending ACL tear. Playing high school football was the goal for many of the boys in youth leagues—although only a handful would end up as starters. As Mike followed his brothers into the sport, his early playing years were marked by interruptions because of his size.

Big for his age, Mike was often forced to "play up," the term used for young players who had to be on teams with older boys because their size or weight prohibited them from playing with their friends. "So when I was in third grade, I could play with some fourth and fifth graders, because I was like ten pounds, twenty pounds heavier than normal people that were my age," Mike says. He remembers he "maxed out" and had to wait until middle school to start playing again.

"I was just this pudgy kid that wanted to play sports and stuff, and I wasn't that cool," he says. The culture at his school in South Parkland, where he lived, emphasized pursuits besides athletics. By the end of elementary school, the people around him were beginning to adopt the dress and attitudes of skater culture, the abbreviated term for skateboarders. He tried adopting the style of dress. "I was posing," he says, recalling his discomfort. Looking at his peers, he would think, "You'll see. I'll be cool eventually."

Although he had resisted playing football, meeting boys like Owen Thomas and Marc Quilling as opponents gave him a glimpse of a community where he felt he might be able to fit in. He knew once they reached middle school, they would play together on a Parkland School District team. "I know those kids are up there and I think I'm like them. I think I'm like them," he told himself. "I hope I am."

While Mike struggled to fit in, Owen often enjoyed being the center of attention at Schnecksville Elementary School. Teachers remembered him not as an athlete, but as a whip-smart student who was capable of working several grade levels ahead of his classmates in math. He also was at home performing in school assemblies, where he took on roles as diverse as the Big Bad Wolf and John Travolta wearing a white disco suit in *Saturday Night Fever*. In Cory Smull Hausman's fifth-grade class, he entertained his classmates with impromptu dancing to the popular tune "Mambo Number Five." But during those years, there was another side to the engaging boy. A tendency toward anger and aggression that worked to his advantage on the playing field sometimes posed problems in school. In second grade, he was asked to participate in an anger management class. His father recalled, "The guidance counselor said, 'The only way we could get Owen to participate was if we told him, 'We need you to participate to help other people.' And that helped Owen to deal with his anger."

His desire to help his classmates manifested itself in other ways: fending off a bully on the playground to protect a female friend or championing an autistic boy on the school bus. As he grew older, it was reflected most profoundly in his role as team captain and in the team-first mentality he brought to the playing field.

|||||||||||||

Boys playing youth football in the 1990s, focused on pursuing their passion on the field, weren't likely to pay attention to two events that foreshadowed something that would define the future of their sport. Years later, the boys and their parents remember nothing about the events that first raised an issue that would become increasingly important for those who grew up on the gridiron. In March 1996, the year before Owen Thomas began playing football, brain specialists, team doctors, and trainers from across the Northeast gathered at Allegheny General Hospital in Pittsburgh for a meeting that was billed as the first attempt to confront issues related to the diagnosis and treatment of sports-related concussions. A neurosurgeon named Joe Maroon, head of the neurosurgery department at Allegheny General Hospital, who volunteered his time consulting as the Pittsburgh Steelers' brain specialist, had used his team connections to pull the meeting together. Physicians presenting at the event testified that players and coaches—not doctors—controlled when players return to a game after a concussion. Players freely admitted playing through pain. Their references to "having their bell rung" were matter-of-fact, reflecting an attitude in which hits to the head were considered a routine part of playing the game. It was no surprise to most attending the summit to learn that coaches resisted pulling valuable players from the lineup because of head trauma—a largely invisible injury.[5]

The second event, on July 26, 1997, appeared completely unrelated to that 1996 conference in Pittsburgh. On that day, former Steeler center Mike Webster was inducted into the Pro Football Hall of Fame in Canton, Ohio. By that time, Webster had been steadily falling apart, mentally and physically.

His former quarterback, Terry Bradshaw, introduced him in Canton with words both passionate and heartfelt. Recalling what he had needed to help him do his job as quarterback, Bradshaw extolled the way that Webster had filled the role. "I said, 'Give me a winner. Give me somebody I can count on,'" Bradshaw said, his voice rising. "Somebody that'll tell me, 'Terry, no, don't run this play.' Somebody who will help me get the team in line. Mike did it. Mike controlled it. We needed him. We used him. We leaned on him. *He was our strength.*"

After the introduction, Webster's rambling, Ritalin-fueled acceptance speech made it clear that Webster was seriously ill.

As he spoke for twenty minutes, his words were often confused. There were moments of lucidity, among them Webster's declaration, "You know, it's painful to play football, obviously. It's not fun out there being in two-a-day drills in the heat of summer and banging heads. It's not a natural thing."[6]

Yet the experiences Webster cited in his speech were exactly those that drew thousands of boys to the game. Football was filled with rituals they equated with coming of age and growing into manhood. The boys longed to be part of the fraternity of young men who survived the drills in the heat, endured the banging heads, and savored victory on the field. And they were willing to do whatever was necessary to be part of it.

CHAPTER 4

IN THE MIDDLE

AT FIRST BOB STECKEL thought he had imagined the sound. It was early on a stifling August morning—the first day of football camp at Orefield Middle School. The pungent smell of dozens of young sweating bodies lingered in the quiet locker room. Steckel, who coached at the middle school and freshman levels for Parkland for twenty-five years, knew it was too early for players to arrive. Yet there was no mistaking the sound: the impatient, staccato taps were the sound of football cleats against the locker room's concrete floor. Looking out of his office to the cinderblock room lined with red metal lockers, he saw Owen sitting on a bench. He was dressed in full uniform with helmet and shoulder pads—apparently unaware that there would be no hitting during the first three days of practice.

"Owen?"

The preteen turned his blue eyes toward Steckel. "What, coach?"

"We're not hitting today."

The words had the effect of a pin popping a balloon. Owen seemed to deflate before him. His shoulders sagged as disappointment registered on every inch of his body. This day, long anticipated, was not going to offer immediate opportunities for the parts of the sport he most enjoyed.

This encounter with Owen was the first glimpse of a player who had the attributes that Steckel says only those who are "genuine football players" possess. "There are kids who like the *idea* of playing football. They like the idea that they're part of a team and that they're wearing the uniform," Steckel says. "But there's the rare kid who loves all aspects of the game. He loves the physicality, he loves the camaraderie. He even loves the intellectual aspects, those X's and O's diagramming the plays. He's emotional on the field."

From his earliest days, Owen Thomas was one of those players. It is why, years later, Steckel would refer to the team from those years, as "Owen's team."

Another disappointment emerged for middle school players on the first day: practices would be held on the baseball field, not on the football field itself. Marc Quilling referred to the practice field as a dust bowl. "Except when it rained. Then it was mud," he says. The boys, eager to graduate to the Trojans' home turf, would have to wait for their first game on the field.

Parkland High School's football stadium sits perched on a hill overlooking Orefield Middle School. Students entering and exiting the building can look up and see the goalposts extending like fingers pointed toward the crisp, blue autumn sky. In fall 2000, seating was being expanded, making it appear even more imposing. As Owen and his friends entered the middle school, the stadium held a promise that their dream of playing high school football would soon be realized.

Football stadiums are usually built close to a school district's high school, a location that affirms the supremacy of the sport as the most valued of all extracurricular activities. In Parkland, its location next to one of the district's two middle schools reflects the school district's burgeoning expansion. As its population soared, a new high school was built to accommodate it, opening in 1999. The original high school, dating back to 1954, became a middle school for students in grades six, seven, and eight. As a result, younger boys already in love with the game of football passed the stadium every day as they entered and exited the school, a reminder that they were closer to becoming Parkland Trojans.[1]

The allure of football for young athletes was strong in the years from 1990 to 2003. As Owen and his teammates grew from boyhood to adolescence, it was the most popular sport for high school boys across the United States. By the time Owen was playing football in middle school in fall 2002, interest in the sport showed no sign of diminishing, with the number of high school football players totaling 1,023,142. It would only keep growing, with the number reaching 1,105,583 by the time he was a senior in high school.[2]

|||||||||||||

Mike Fay had anticipated being able to play on a team with players like Owen Thomas, Marc Quilling, and Jamie Pagliaro. In middle school, they transitioned from being rivals in youth football to teammates on the middle school squad. Other teammates—among them Mike Parkhill, Eric Rueda, Phil Bortz, and Hesham Abdelaal—joined them. Mike and other boys would be bused from Springhouse Middle School to practices in Orefield. For many of the eager seventh graders, their dedication and passion for the sport was stoked by the example set by older siblings. Mike's brother Joey had played with Owen's brother Matt on Parkland High School's 1996 championship football team. "We saw us as continuing that legacy. We knew that we had to be top dogs, like they were," Mike says. The boys never doubted that they would follow in their brothers' footsteps.

Playing in middle school meant the boys were beginning another, more serious level of play. The focus in the North and South Parkland youth leagues was developmental, emphasizing skill building. That changed as they entered middle school, when an emphasis was placed on preparing players for the physicality of the sport. A strength and conditioning program with weight lifting was introduced. Summer practices were more rigorous, and for the first time the boys were exposed to doubles—two practices, one in morning and one in afternoon. Some days found the boys doing bear crawls in hundred-degree heat. Crouching with arms extended, they placed their hands on the ground and, with knees bent, propelled themselves forward, alternating hands and feet like bruins moving through a forest. Sweat poured down their faces.

Adapting to the tougher physical demands was not easy for some of the boys. The increased rigor in practice didn't come naturally to Mike Fay. When the team first had to run laps during workouts, Mike stood on the sidelines and cried. "I can't do it," he said. His father, standing at the fence to watch his youngest son's progress, added to the pressure. The summer heat at preseason practices also took its toll. Sometimes Mike vomited so much that coaches considered sending him to the hospital. On one occasion, Owen stood over him.

"You're letting the team down. You have to fight through this," Owen cajoled him.

"He had that sense that you had to fight through adversity," says Mike, who was an offensive lineman. Owen espoused the kind of commitment that leads athletes to stay in the game after jarring impacts should sideline them. Researchers who have studied the incidence of concussions and other injuries in all sports note that many committed athletes continue playing after they are hurt. Playing through pain is a badge of honor among athletes of all ages, the sign of a competitor who is willing to risk personal well-being for the sake of winning. Although the mind-set has come under increasing criticism, especially for young athletes, it was an accepted sign of dedication and commitment nearly twenty years ago, when Owen and his friends first played football.

Middle school also was the time when the boys began settling into the positions they would play for the rest of their careers. In seventh grade, Marc, already established as a quarterback in youth football, attended the fabled Curry Quarterback Camp in Berwick, Pennsylvania. Founded by the late coach George Curry—the winningest high school coach in Pennsylvania history, with 455 career wins—the camp has prepared many young quarterbacks for success. Going to the camp at age twelve, Marc was far from the youngest player there. Boys as young as nine go to the camp to be groomed to quarterback their teams. Attending such sports camps has become a significant part of youth sports in the United States. The one-day Curry camp costs a modest $50 to $60[3] per player, compared to $1,500 and more at weeklong camps that some young athletes attend.[4] The pricey camps promise young players a boost to their skills in the coming season and hint at long-term payoffs in the form of college athletic scholarships.

Marc was not the only athlete laying the groundwork for the rest of his playing career. Starting in middle school, Owen did what few players manage, playing both offense and defense as a fullback and linebacker. He also began fulfilling another role that his teammates would come to expect from him in years ahead: that of self-appointed motivator who would encourage other players, urging them to give their best. His encouragement could be gentle. On the first day in the middle school weight room, Mike Parkhill watched as his longtime friend easily did reps lifting 135 pounds. Trying to bench 95 pounds, Mike was nearly crushed by the bar. Owen calmly walked over to him. "Don't worry, Park; everyone's gotta start somewhere," Owen said. Mike Parkhill remembered the moment on Owen's birthday, five years after his friend died, and commemorated it on his Facebook page.

Mike Fay says, "Owen got to be the best kid on the team as a seventh grader. No matter how old he was, he was always the best. In middle school, we saw him as a leader—but I didn't want to let him know that."

Football was not the only thing drawing their attention as they entered middle school.

Cheerleaders had been around since the boys began playing youth football, when even peewee teams had their own cheering squad. At that age, the girls were merely part of the landscape at games. In junior high, their presence came into sharper focus as the boys naturally became more aware of the opposite sex. Although girls had been guaranteed equal access to opportunities to play sports after the passage of Title IX in 1972, Parkland had no female football players during the years Owen and his friends were Trojans. It was very much the traditional separation of boys on the field, girls on the sidelines cheering them on.

Owen had met Abbie and Jess Benner before they became middle-school classmates. His brother, Morgan, was friends with their older brother, Nick. The girls are twins—not identical, but very nearly alike in appearance and stature. The sisters are friendly and chatty, sometimes finishing each other's sentences. Jess and Abbie's good friend, Emily Toth, was also a cheerleader and had known Owen since elementary school. Soon he became a welcome fourth wheel when the three girls congregated after school.

"We were the same age, so then we went into middle school together. . . . And then we just clicked. Right away, we hung out," Abbie says.

Jess interjects, "All the time."

Abbie laughs. "*All* the time!"

Although the toughest of players, Owen became a different person off the field—the kind of guy that girls quickly adopt as a friend. He often joined the three girls at one of their houses to spend hours playing *Dance Dance Revolution*, a popular Japanese arcade game that introduced a home video game version in the late 1990s. Players at home stepped on a plastic mat in patterns corresponding to arrows appearing on the video game screen. Steps were done to the beat of music, and players were rated on the accuracy of the series of steps they executed making up their "dance." Owen was competitive even when playing a video dance game, always striving to win. The girls frequently dissolved into laughter at the intensity of the competition.

"He was our protector," Abbie recalls. "He was always there. He always looked out for us."

Despite his reputation as everyone's buddy, Owen developed an early romantic interest in Abbie.

"When we were in sixth grade—do you really count that? We were technically boyfriend and girlfriend for a little bit, but I don't know how much dating you do in sixth grade. We were together for a little bit," Abbie says, blushing.

The crush that started in middle school never diminished for Owen, even though both would go on to date others, before rekindling their relationship in high school.

The year that the boys were in eighth grade, the middle school team went undefeated. By the end of the season, they also had the distinction of having no points scored against them. In the final game of that season, against Easton at Cottingham Stadium, Owen established himself as an aggressive player who comes through at a critical juncture in the game.

"Owen was running the ball, and he's coming up the sideline and there's one guy that tried to tackle him. And boom! He hit him! And then another guy, and he hit *that* guy. And then a third guy," Steckel recalls. "It was just a classic run. It's something we practiced, but you never thought you'd actually see it done to that extent." They lost the game on an intercepted pass—the season's only loss.

In fall 2002, as Owen Thomas and the Parkland players were eighth graders, playing on an undefeated middle school football team, they were preparing to do what they'd dreamt of doing since they first suited up on a peewee team: play high school football. Football was forever and none of them could imagine the future without it. It was the thing they loved the most.

|||||||||||||

As it did for the Parkland boys, football became part of Mike Webster's life from an early age. Long before Webster became a Hall of Fame center for the Pittsburgh Steelers, his father remembered him watching the Green Bay Packers as a child and saying he'd play for the team someday. Later, at Rhinelander High School in rural Oneida County, Wisconsin, he played football for the Hodags—named for a mythical Northwoods creature. The game became an escape from the grueling work on his father's potato farm and, later, a family business digging water wells. Webster would take castoffs, like pieces of pipe from the well business, and turn them into strength-training equipment. He was lifting twice a day by the time he was a senior in high school.[5]

Going on to play for the University of Wisconsin Badgers, he anchored the team's offensive line and was captain as a senior. His rigorous weight training would help earn him accolades as the Big Ten's best center. He was drafted by the Pittsburgh Steelers because of his hard-hitting play and quickness, but he was considered small for an offensive lineman in the NFL at six feet, two-and-a-half inches, and 225 pounds. At the end of his rookie season, when the Steelers won the first Super Bowl in the team's history, he vowed to return bigger and stronger. When he checked into training camp the next August, he weighed in between 250 and 260 pounds. It was the result of a regimen of weight gain and "bulking up" that even younger players on the high school level often are urged to emulate in the pursuit of being bigger and stronger on the field.

Although Webster later admitted to some steroid use before the drugs were outlawed, his increased mass also could be attributed to a training schedule that most described as obsessive. It included off-season powerlifting with guys who could bench press five hundred pounds. At home, he did lunges with a barbell behind his head in the snow in his backyard, where he also kept a blocking sled for off-season workouts at 6 a.m.[6]

During a sixteen-year professional career, he earned the nickname Iron Mike. From his sophomore year in high school until he ended his career playing for the Kansas City Chiefs, he estimated that he'd played three hundred out of his teams' three hundred games. There were other reasons for the nickname.

Webster was known for using his head as a weapon, driving it into opponents as he came off the line. Over the years, a visible layer of scar tissue built up at the spot where his helmet pushed into advancing linemen. Yet there were only two references related to head injuries in his medical records during his playing career, and there were no diagnosed concussions. Part of Webster's legend as Iron Mike included an incident when he checked himself out of the hospital to go play at Pittsburgh's Three Rivers Stadium. As it was for most players, playing through pain was a badge of honor.[7]

When he walked away from football at age thirty-eight, it was as if he walked away from life. The twelve years after his 1990 retirement were a slow unraveling, as if football had somehow held it all together and, without it, life fell apart. There were mood swings, angry outbursts, bankruptcy. It was reported that he'd sold his Super Bowl rings. His marriage ended. At one point Webster was living in his car. His health had deteriorated, and he was charged with forging prescriptions for the drug Ritalin, which he used to help him focus. In 2002, he was hospitalized for a heart attack. After surgery for two blocked arteries, his body, subjected to so much trauma on the playing field, began to shut down. He died at age fifty.[8]

A Steelers fan working in the coroner's office brought Webster's case to the attention of Bennet Omalu, a Nigerian doctor working there who had been mentored by legendary Allegheny County coroner Cyril Wecht. Wecht had made a name for himself by weighing in on celebrity deaths and had advanced the idea that John F. Kennedy had not been killed by a lone gunman. Like his mentor, Omalu was brilliant and flamboyant, a doctor who wore expensive suits and who boasted a long list of degrees and credentials. Besides his medical degree, he'd earned a master's degree in public health and an MBA. He had fellowship training in forensic pathology and neuropathology.[9] Football players were outside of Omalu's frame of reference, and he famously asked, "Who's Mike Webster?" when his colleague asked him to perform the autopsy. Everything seemed routine, but Omalu decided to ask Wecht for permission to study the brain in more depth. In examining it, he found an unusual buildup of tau protein. It was the kind of buildup found in boxers that went with the condition called "dementia pugilistica," or "punch-drunk syndrome." Omalu knew he had discovered something important. He sought confirmation of his diagnosis from two renowned neuropathologists at University of Pittsburgh Medical Center, Dr. Ronald Hamilton and Dr. Steve DeKosky. Omalu had studied with Hamilton. De-Kosky headed UPMC's Department of Neurology. Both men corroborated Omalu's findings. He named the condition that he had discovered "chronic traumatic encephalopathy." Later, it would be abbreviated as CTE. The findings were reported in a July 2005 article titled "Chronic Traumatic Encephalopathy in a National Football League Player" in the journal *Neurosurgery*.[10]

Omalu thought it would be deemed a groundbreaking discovery by the medical community. He naively thought it would be embraced by the National Football League. But what Omalu did not initially realize was that the discovery would also be important to boys playing middle school football.

CHAPTER 5

FOOTBALL BOYS

THE SUN BURNS OFF the early-morning haze leaving a blanket of August heat hanging over the practice fields. The Parkland High School Trojans exit the locker room in a wave, trotting across the parking lots that separate the high school from the practice fields. Cleats clack on hot black macadam as they approach three descending, green-terraced fields bordering busy Cedar Crest Boulevard.

Summer is short for high school football players. Less than two months separate the end of the school year in June from preseason practice in August. For the dedicated ones, there really is no break. The summer months are spent conditioning in the weight room to ensure being in the best possible shape when practice starts again. There's no room for much else. Working a summer job, maybe, or playing video games and hanging out with the guys. Those things come behind lifting, workouts, and, eventually, preseason practice.

Workouts that had seemed insurmountable in middle school were almost welcome now. For players like Owen and his friends, it was a privilege to be part of the summertime ritual of off-season conditioning and drills in ninety-degree heat. He and his friends had watched older brothers, friends, and neighbors play as Parkland Trojans. When it was their turn, they savored it all.

The team held preseason practice every weekday in August from 8 a.m. to noon under the unforgiving summer sun. During the years that Owen and his friends were Trojans, two-a-days were part of the regimen. It meant daily practice time was doubled, with players returning to continue the workouts in the stifling late afternoon heat.

The tradition of two-a-days has disappeared from many high school football programs—although many, particularly in the South, still cling to the practice. Limiting full contact to just one of the two practices is becoming standard. (Contact practices are those in which tackling and hitting are part of the routine.) Two-a-days were banished in 2011 under the NFL collective bargaining agreement because some felt it had become almost a form of professional hazing.[1] The National Collegiate Athletic Association (NCAA) in 2017 decreed that only walk-throughs—no contact or conditioning, no helmets and pads—would be permitted at second practices held the same day. Even then, three hours had to separate the two practices, to give players time to recover.[2] At Parkland High School in 2006, two-a-days were routine, a part of the football culture to be both endured and savored.

Summer practices for the Trojans followed a pattern as carefully planned and well-executed as military drills. First came training supervised by the special teams coordinator—ten minutes in the morning, with ten minutes in the afternoon during double sessions. In that brief time, skills were polished for game kickoffs, punting, and kicking for the extra point in a field goal.

Players, more than a hundred of them, were broken into three groups. Freshmen, clad in black jerseys, practiced together on a field adjacent to the busy road that runs by the high school. Varsity and junior varsity players in red jerseys spent time on the neighboring fields working on individual skills before coming together for group and teamwork later.

Coaches barked directions at lagging runners. Players chanted as they rotated to the next drill: "One, two, three, crap!"

Bodies thudded, making contact with tackling dummies, the hits punctuated by guttural grunts. Underscoring it all was the subtle hum of insects in the tall grass ringing the field, like a chorus of ghostly fans.

On the middle practice field, running backs and receivers engaged in drills. A boy ran, caught a pass, rolled to the ground and sprang to his feet, moving seamlessly in a choreographed dance that became part of body memory.

In the field dubbed "the hole"—so named because it is the lowest of the three practice fields—linemen worked on fundamentals of offensive and defensive play. They took turns pushing against sleds, a piece of equipment shaped like a snow sled standing upright. It allowed them to refine the moves needed to drive back opponents. Later players might face off against each other or run at tackling dummies.

"It's gotta come from you," exhorted one of the line coaches. "Me standing here yelling like a fucking idiot is not going to do it. It's got to come from you."

Under his admonitions, players picked up the pace. In the center field, they practiced an intricate drill of cutting and running. "Hard right, soft left," a coach intoned. Players moved almost hypnotically to his chanted directions. A big kid wielding a camera ran between groups of players capturing their moves for later analysis. At regular intervals, someone ordered, "Go take a drink," a safeguard against dangerous dehydration. Players refreshed themselves from the arc of water streaming from a black hose at the edge of the field.

Standing on a hill overlooking it all, head coach Jim Morgans studied the action with the concentration of a general watching troop movements in times of war. Sometimes he uttered words of praise—"Good one!" Other times, he was the disciplinarian: "Don't talk back to me. I get enough of that from my kids." Graying, sporting a dab of a goatee in the center of his chin, he strode across the field in shorts, a baseball cap shielding his eyes from the sun.

Morgans was born in Wilkes-Barre, Pennsylvania, a small, gritty city in the coal regions north of the affluent Pennsylvania suburb where he coached. His father worked for the Central Railroad of New Jersey, known as the Jersey Central, on the trains hauling coal from the mines in northeastern Pennsylvania to where it was distributed in Philadelphia and New Jersey. Catholic school was a given for Jim and his siblings, who belonged to a family of devout Catholics. Also a given: he would transfer to Wilkes-Barre's public E. L. Meyers High School when he was old enough, so he could play football. Morgans's father had followed the same path in his youth. A picture frame hangs in Coach Morgans's house, which he points to with pride. It contains four photos: One is of his father, in a football jersey—W-B for Wilkes-Barre in giant letters on the front. The other three photos are of Morgans and his two sons, Billy and Jimmy, all taken in uniform at various stages of their playing careers. Morgans, like many of his players, is part of a family of football players.

Morgans began playing after his family moved south to Allentown, in Pennsylvania's Lehigh Valley, due to his father's railroad work. The younger Morgans was a lineman for Allentown Central Catholic High School's Vikings. From that time, football governed his life choices. West Texas State University lured him to Cisco Junior College, now Cisco College, to play with the thought that he'd move on to the university after two years. But another offer, from Louisiana College, a Baptist school in Pineville, Louisiana, drew him to play for its Wildcats team. Morgans's record there would earn him a place in the school's athletic hall of fame.

During his college years, Morgans's roommate was an African American football player named John Love. On team trips, players sometimes went to the movies on free nights. It was the 1960s, and segregation was still a reality in the South, so Black players were consigned to sit in the balcony while their white teammates could sit on the main floor of the theater.

Morgans joined John Love in the balcony. After graduation, Morgans taught briefly at a southern high school, but missed home and returned north. Soon after joining the faculty at his alma mater, Allentown Central Catholic, he began his coaching career. It had an inauspicious start, for his first seven years at the school. But after leaving Central Catholic and working with other head coaches at Muhlenberg College and Parkland, Morgans returned to Central a seasoned coach. In a memorable ten-season run, between 1989 and 1998, Morgans led Central Catholic to a 94–20 record, with six District 11 championships and five East Penn Conference crowns. It cemented his reputation as a top coach. Including his earlier stint at the school from 1976 to 1981, Morgans compiled an overall 115–76–1 record at Central Catholic.[3]

He was wooed away by two other school districts before landing back at Parkland in 2005. His winning ways and amiable personality made him something of a local celebrity among sports fans in the community. His seven children are used to being identified as his offspring; one of his daughters good-naturedly complains about how often she's asked, "Is Jim Morgans your dad?"

The unpretentious demeanor stemming from Morgans's working-class background stayed with him. He has a straightforward way of talking to everyone, from parents to players. People know where they stand with Coach Morgans. Parents warm to his coaching style, which rewards both star athletes and second-stringers. Morgans names a player of the week—awarding a star decal that players paste on their helmets. Players don't have to see playing time to win it. "The worst player on the football team is still important. He's important," Morgans states unequivocally. "If he gives us a great practice, we're going to point him out. He may not play, may not be in on Friday night, but he's there. What makes a kid stay there, and go through that grind? What makes a kid do that, that he's one of sixty players, but he never really gets in the game? He's a senior, he's been with you for four years. I love those kids. They're fantastic."

||||||||||||

Joining the Parkland program when Owen and his friends were juniors, Coach Morgans inherited a group of players who displayed the moxie and commitment that head coaches prize. They would go undefeated in fall 2006, during their senior year.

They were a team committed to the hard work and dedication that Morgans required. After summer practices ended and the season began, football was a six-day-a-week commitment. Monday practices were walk-throughs, with coaches focused on reviewing the strengths and weaknesses of that week's opposing team. On Tuesdays and Wednesdays, the team ran plays and drills. Thursday was another walk-through, before the game on Friday night. On Saturdays, players gathered to watch the game film from the night before and previewed film of the next week's opponent. Saturdays also included time for lifting and running. Sundays were the sole day off before the routine started all over again on Monday.

"When the season ends, they get off until Christmas, and then in January we start in the weight room and lift. If they don't lift, they're going to get left behind. They have to love it," Morgans says. He pauses and a half-smile crosses his face, his expression changing from military general to that of a benevolent father figure. "And they do love it."

It was never a question that football came first for Owen Thomas and the Parkland Trojans of 2005 and 2006.

"That's the way it is with football boys," former Parkland cheerleader Jess Benner quips. She was Mike Fay's girlfriend while her twin, Abbie, dated Owen. Football boys, Jess explains, are bound by their love of the game and by their close relationships. Running together like a pack of sleek, fit young animals, they share inside jokes, play endless rounds of *Call of Duty* in basement rec rooms, and surreptitiously chew tobacco. Being a football boy was their identity, one that grew slowly, starting when they played peewee ball. If you were the girlfriend of a football boy, you got used to sharing him with an entire team.

"Our girlfriends used to get mad at us for not spending more time with them," Mike Fay recalls ruefully. "They'd say, 'Didn't you just see them?' And we'd say, 'Yeah, but that was yesterday.'"

The girls were seeing a dynamic that has been key in the lives of boys and young men in America: the brotherhood. The relationships, shared experiences, and adventures of boys and men define a brotherhood for its members. It is such an important part of the development of boys in American society that psychologist Michael C. Reichert devotes a chapter to examining it in his book *How to Raise a Boy: The Power of Connection to Build Good Men.* Brotherhood is built into the formal and informal institutions that are part of boys' growing up years: Boy Scouts, athletic teams, even groups of boys that gather on playgrounds. In some cases, it can exert a negative influence, such as the dynamic found in gang violence or fraternity hazing. But in many cases—such as among Owen and the other football boys—being a member of a brotherhood becomes the ultimate manifestation of the exhortation "I have your back." It provides a sense of belonging and gives young men a place where they can feel free to express affection for one another.

Coach Morgans set the tone for expressing affection among team members. "Because of the nature of the game, you've got to be tough . . . but never leave the field without letting them know . . . and I have told them . . . that you love them. Because the nature of the game just brings you together."

The world of the football boy was built around rituals and rites invisible to the rest of the world. One of them—learning to chew tobacco—was part of the initiation for those playing on the Parkland varsity team. Owen, Mike, and Marc played varsity as sophomores—a rare privilege that only the most talented players at Parkland achieved. Mike remembers Owen's older brother Morgan, a Parkland Hall of Fame player, tossing him the tin of chew one day in the locker room. "And he said, 'Fay, you want to be on the varsity line, you gotta try this.' I put some in my mouth. Of course, I got really dizzy. And I almost threw up."

Eventually Owen started chewing too—"After saying 'no' about twenty times," Mike recalls. Once he started, Owen rapidly coined his own vocabulary to talk about the habit. In Owen's parlance, the last remnants of tobacco in a tin—too small for a full pinch—became a "taste bud tickler." In a maneuver he called "the flip," Owen turned over the chaw in his mouth, reversing the side held against his teeth to extract the maximum amount of tobacco juice.

Those words were part of a language particular to the football boys, much of it invented by Owen with help from Mike. "Charleston Chaw-daddy chew" accompanied the passing of the chewing tobacco tin. "My brotha" became their special salutation, one that began in the locker room and would be repeated in hundreds of posts on social media for years after. "Owen was known for his lingo," Marc Quilling recalls. The unique language invented by Owen and Mike migrated from the practice field and locker room into the classrooms and halls of the high school. After they studied Shakespeare's *Macbeth* in tenth grade, the boys traveled through the halls between classes, clucking like chickens, "Mac-Mac-Macbeth."

The boys seldom addressed each other by their given names. Relationships were cemented by bestowing nicknames, and Owen was the expert at inventing monikers. Some evolved from abbreviating a name: Marc Quilling became Quill and Jamie Pagliaro was Pags. Last names too short to be abbreviated were used in place of first names—with Mike Fay becoming Fay and Chris Funk known simply as Funk. Nicknaming extended beyond the boys to girls in their circle, with Owen doing a "Name Game" riff. The result was Kristen Dota becoming Dotes Ma-dotes and Irina Levin dubbed Ree-ner Schnitzel.

Those were traditions established in fun. On game days, they took a serious turn. Every warrior has his ritual before battle, a series of observances meant to guarantee victory. In football, it's often an amalgam of mental preparation and superstition. Before each game, Owen would sit alone at the far end of the hall in the athletic wing of the high school, back against the lockers, eyes closed. The moments of quiet contemplation yielded a focused, trash-talking fighter on the offensive line. "He'd be there telling players, 'I'm coming for you. Coming for you,'" Marc recalls. Players on the opposing team were wary of the redheaded Viking, knowing he was capable of backing up his words with action.

Marc, wearing number 15 at quarterback, had his own series of pregame rites. He would warm up wearing black sweatpants. "Then I'd take them off and give them to Coach Lane and he'd wear them on the sidelines," Quill says.

The superstitions at times bordered on the ridiculous. "Before every game, Chris Funk, Mike Parkhill, and me would have to sing [songs by] Panic! At the Disco," Pags says. "Then they would have to touch Mike's flat foot."

Even the coaches would succumb to superstition. Parkland defensive coach Ryan Hulmes plucked stones from near the stadium and tucked them in his pocket to take to away games, carrying a bit of home field advantage with him.

Some rituals were a shared experience for team members. On Thursday nights before Friday games, Owen and his friends would gather at their classmate Matt Bergstein's house for another team ritual. His band, A Crisis Andrea, would give a private performance. Mike said, "We went to his house and got a heavy metal show."

||||||||||||

Next to actually playing the game, good times in the weight room ranked high with the football boys. Located in the high school's athletic wing, it was a place for strenuous workouts and bonding with guys who were serious about football. The long, brightly lit room has cinderblock walls painted in the school colors of scarlet and silver-gray. A huge head of a Trojan warrior is depicted in profile on one wall, the helmet topped with a bright red plume. Another mural shows the Trojan in a full body pose, brandishing a shield bearing the school district logo. Beside him, the years of Parkland's state championship teams are emblazoned on the wall.

Mirrors reflect the bodies of athletes working out. The room is packed with more than a half-dozen weight-lifting stations, each set up to serve lifters of different ability levels. Stationary bikes and treadmills form a line like mechanical sentries. Racks of dumbbells stand ready. Speakers spew an earsplitting soundtrack of heavy metal music.

For Owen and friends, every day was a party in the weight room. During a typical session, Mike cranked up the volume on the sound system and the first chords of AC/DC's "Thunderstruck" filled the room. Owen, clad in his favorite Led Zeppelin shirt, leaped into the air off the black bench where he'd just finished lifting, his long red hair streaming like streaks of fire behind him. He and Mike stood next to each other, Owen strumming air guitar as he tossed his head back and forth. Mike followed suit. Around the room, other players paused between reps, grinning at their antics. Facing each other, they engaged in an air guitar standoff, faces contorted, heads jerking in time to the beat.

When the next song launched—Led Zeppelin's "Whole Lotta Love"—more guys joined in. First Pags, then Hesham. Pretty soon, half a dozen of the Trojans' toughest players were engaging in imaginary drumming, strumming invisible six-strings, carried along by the relentless beat of vocalist Robert Plant, guitarist Jimmy Page, bassist John Paul Jones, and drummer John Bonham. For a few minutes, the boys became the band.

During a pause in the music some of the guys who had been watching applauded and cheered. Owen grinned under his bright yellow bandana, catching his breath, as Mike high-fived him.

It was weight lifting, Owen Thomas style. "We'd be absolute fools in the weight room," Mike says, shaking his head at the memory.

Jamie remembers when Coach Bob Ruisch, then brand new, walked into the weight room for the first time. "He walked in the door, and we all were just playing our air guitars and drums and stuff. Not goofing off: we were serious about working out. But he saw me and Owen and Mike Fay and Marc and he was like, 'Oh, yeah, this is where I want to be,'" Jamie says. "We knew how to have fun, but at the same time, the coaches knew we were there for one thing and that was to get better and win football games."

For many players, lifting weights was something that was required. For Owen, as with so many of his interests, it was a passion. Players were required to lift four days a week off-season and twice a week during the season. Owen held himself to a rigorous schedule, coming to school at 6 a.m. to hit the weight room before his first class. In Diane Cortazzo's first-period German honors class, the teacher known as "Frau" chided him for putting his head on the desk. "I said, 'Owen, what are you doing?' He explained that he was physically exhausted from lifting; he wasn't sleeping. He told me, 'Frau, I hear everything you're saying. Call on me anytime.' I would call on him and he would lift his head up and give me the right answer. Most kids, if their head was on the desk, it meant they weren't listening."

In the weight room, he'd be on the first rack—the rack for the strongest lifters. By the time he was a senior, he could bench press three hundred pounds and squat lift five hundred. That kind of strength was important for a lineman, whose job is to stop opposing players in their relentless drive down the field. "Owen was really good at dead lifts," Marc remembers, using a powerlifting term in which a weight lifter takes the weight from the floor to waist height in one motion.

With many linemen in the pros and at Division I colleges topping three hundred pounds, the bar is set high. Players are bigger and more powerful than they have ever been in the history of the game. University of Nebraska professor Timothy Gay studies the physics of football. He notes that linemen's weights from 1920 to the present have increased from one hundred and ninety pounds to more than three hundred. That's a 50 percent increase in a football player's body mass leading to an equally significant increase in the force players exert on the field.[4] Players today must have both strength and size to compete. Owen worked relentlessly to achieve both.

Owen's father, Tom, recalls, "He wanted to be heavier. He made himself gain. It wasn't his natural weight. Morgan didn't have to try to gain weight. Owen had to push himself. He played at 240 and he was about six two, so he was big. But he was not naturally big. He had a different physique." He would worry about losing weight, Tom says.

Owen's preoccupation with weight gain led him to develop an appetite unequaled among his friends. "He was a little vacuum cleaner. Anything girls didn't want to eat at lunch, he would vacuum it up," his mother says. "Even the lunch ladies gave him extra."

His preoccupation with size is common among many young athletes. Athletes brag about consuming five thousand calories and more a day to maintain a playing weight. Although Owen adopted a high-calorie diet, some athletes take more extreme measures, using dietary supplements or even experimenting with steroids. The push to be as large as possible among high school football players can lead to unhealthy outcomes. Results of a study published in 2007 in the *Journal of the American Medical Association* showed that, among 3,600 high school linemen in Iowa, 45 percent of the players were overweight and 9 percent were obese.

Size brought an ability to intimidate, and that is what Owen and his teammates wanted to do—intimidate. Jamie Pagliaro says Owen succeeded. "He was feared, because he was aggressive. He was just everywhere. He was just all over the field," Pagliaro says.

Owen's high school coaches remember him as a physical player. "In the vernacular that we use, he was a bender," Morgans says, describing the stance used by the best defensive players, who bend their knees, distributing their weight to give them more power to drive back the offense.

His passion inspired his high school teammates, just as it had done in middle school. Owen—already team captain as a junior—drove his peers to be their best. They emulated his work ethic in the weight room and on the field. But his charismatic presence and ability to deliver a pep talk was equally powerful.

"When we were walking out onto that field for pre-practice, he knew exactly what to say," Pags recalls. "He was always the football player I looked up to. I've played with some really good football players. He wasn't always the most talented, but he had the heart to play the game, more than anyone I've ever met. He was unbelievable on the field. He was a leader. I think that was his biggest attribute."

||||||||||||

The Parkland football boys' nostalgia for their time together extended beyond the moments shared on the field. The times shared off the field secured their bond and defined their friendships as the most important ones in their young lives.

"We look back now with such fondness," Mike says. "As you get older, you realize that's over, that's gone—that little three-year blurb [*sic*]. And you look back and you think, how could three years matter so much?" He pauses, shaking his head. "Those three years are so important." Those were the years when their identities as athletes solidified and belonging to a brotherhood of players on a team became an indelible part of their lives.

On one memorable September night, just before summer slipped into fall, there was no football game, no practice to demand the football boys' disciplines. On a rare night off, John Zaccaro, another Parkland linebacker, sat with Owen on the deck at the Thomases' house on Jonagold Road, facing a bank of pine trees that rimmed the yard, like sentinels watching the suburban neighborhood. Dusk fell, dropping its blanket of dark over the backyard, slowly at first, then more quickly as the sun lowered in the sky. The two young men enjoyed a moment of companionable silence, killing time before meeting up with the rest of the crew. Suddenly the darkness was punctuated with a net of fireflies flashing like tiny Christmas lights across the pines, hundreds of them sparkling against the trees from one end of the yard to the other.

"Damn! Do you see that?" John asked, breaking the silence.

"Yeah," Owen said.

They slipped back into silence until John's cell phone rang and they set off. That night would be like many others, John says. "We would pick up two or three guys in my SUV," he recalls. They moved from house to house, hanging out, having fun. Sometimes it was at Owen's place for endless hours playing video games. Other times they traveled to Chris Funk's barn on Gaskill Road for beer that tasted best because they were too young to be drinking it.

Their favorite hideout was the Zaccaros' home in nearby Northampton.

"That was the real country wooded place out in the middle of nowhere," Mike Fay says, his eyes gleaming with the joy of remembered good times and harmless hellraising. "You'd leave, just say, 'Dad, I'll be gone for two days.' Once you got there, you knew no one was going to come looking for you; no one was going to catch you and yell at you."

The boys would hang out in a shed and in a gazebo overlooking the woods. Often they built bonfires. There was always beer. And it was there that the group smoked marijuana for the first time, hurriedly extinguishing the joint when Mrs. Zaccaro came out to ask if they'd like some spaghetti.

Her cooking was always a highlight. The boys love talking about the time she made a giant tub of sloppy joes and Owen stood eating right out of the pot using a dripping ladle to spoon the tangy meat as the guys chortled and laughed around him.

High school was a time, John says, of "innocent awesomeness." It was a time to be football boys.

Coach Morgans says that Owen and his friends seemed aware of the unique time in their lives, even as they were experiencing it. "Every game to them was a special event. It was like they knew that this wasn't going to last. They knew it. It was a treasure that they could participate and play football in high school."

Three years later, when Owen was at the University of Pennsylvania, laboring in the intense atmosphere at the Wharton School of the University of Pennsylvania, he would remember those times, telling his high school friends that he felt lonely in the city.

After he chose to fasten a football belt around his neck and hang himself, his friends wondered if he had thought of their times together in his last moments. If he saw, as the belt forced the breath out of his body, the lights of a thousand fireflies rising in the gathering darkness.

CHAPTER 6

THUNDERCATS

THE NEW PARKLAND HIGH SCHOOL was dubbed the Taj Mahal when it opened in 1999. The huge school sitting on 128 acres matches the expectations of residents in the upwardly mobile community it serves, with facilities that are the biggest and best of any school in the region. Its three thousand-plus students jam the halls, moving between classes in a school that has a reputation for being an academic and social pressure cooker. Students' cars in the parking lots reflect the socioeconomic diversity of the owners.

Dropped into the sea of Parkland students, Owen Thomas, with his trademark red hair, floated to the top. The school's culture pigeonholed students into myriad social groups: jocks, goths, nerds, brainiacs, bandos, arts kids. Owen navigated among these groups with ease, claiming friends throughout the school.

"He never cared where you came from, what you looked like, who you were," says Parkland teammate John Zaccaro, recalling the way his friend ignored the high school caste system. "He always was nice—unless you were playing against him on the football field in a different color uniform."

Status based on clothes and material possessions seemed meaningless to Owen. His ancient blue Chevy Lumina—dubbed the Lum-dizzle—clearly placed him among the less affluent. His collection of shirts from the Salvation Army was worn as confidently as his peers wore clothes with labels from Abercrombie and Gap. But he and his friends had claimed something more valuable than material possessions to define them in the Parkland culture: they were athletes. More importantly, they were football players—perhaps the most desirable of all the school's social groups.

Mike Fay says the football player identity shaped him from the time he was the awkward kid who wandered the golf course until he became a respected part of the offensive line as a Parkland Trojan. "I got the Life of the Party award, which is an award they give at the end of the year," Mike says. He's so astonished by the fact, he repeats it. "I got the Life of the Party award, and I graduated with nine hundred kids. . . . I don't really like the term, but I guess I became popular. But I felt very lonely and isolated when I was younger."

Being a football player was a shared identity. Getting to wear your football jersey in school on game day Fridays placed you among a brotherhood of sixty or more guys all wearing the same jersey. It was great to be part of the club. In Parkland, the proud football tradition was shared even by the school district's senior administration. High school principal Rich Sniscak coached the Trojans for seven years, winning two district titles, before becoming principal in 2001. In 2011, he would become the school district's superintendent.[1]

Athletes weren't the only students lionized in Parkland. The school also elevated the academically talented, and competition among those students could be as tough as it was among athletes on the playing field. In each year's graduating class, the race to see who would be valedictorian and salutatorian—those graduates with the highest grades—became a face-off among a handful of students whose grade point averages were separated by a hundredth of a point. The district finally eliminated class rank in 2012, five years after Owen and his teammates graduated. With some 56 percent of Parkland students earning averages of 3.0 or better, class rank could actually work against them when applying to college. Because so many had high averages, students with a 4.00 could actually rank below the top 10 percent of the graduating class—the position valued by competitive universities.[2]

Owen's inherent competitiveness helped him to deal with the academic pressure at the high school. Not content to be known only for athletic prowess, he pursued top grades, taking honors and Advanced Placement classes. When his buddies on the team asked him to hang out, the answer invariably was, "After I've done my homework." But unlike many of his classmates who focused on academics, Owen maintained a sense of fun. Steve Yoder, a former Parkland social studies teacher and basketball coach, saw it when the redhead was in his Advanced Placement government class.

Yoder routinely stood at the classroom door to greet students at the start of each class period. One day he looked down the hall to see Owen come around the corner wearing an AC/DC T-shirt, long red hair skimming his shoulders and a small drum set hanging off his arm. Following him was a ragtag group of students, a mix of every different kind of kid in the school.

"What is this mess?" Yoder asked as Owen reached the door.

"You said I could bring it in," Owen said matter-of-factly.

And then Yoder remembered: Owen had lobbied every day during the term that the class should be allowed to play *Guitar Hero*, a popular video game. Yoder had put him off: "You can bring it in on the last day at your last class."

Yoder had forgotten, but when the day came, Owen had remembered. Minutes after he arrived, a full rock band was playing in the classroom, surrounded by laughing students.

"Owen was part of that intense, highly competitive culture at Parkland. A lot of kids who went through there, it impacted their experience. It's great to be an AP student, but it's also great to enjoy being eighteen, seventeen, sixteen. So many kids there didn't experience that. Owen always did," Yoder says. "Intellectually, he was near the top of his class. I had kids who got perfect scores on SATs, who were going to Harvard and Yale. What made Owen different than everyone else was that he was so well adjusted. He balanced it so well."

For others in Parkland, Yoder says, it wasn't so easy. "I felt that at Parkland, there were a lot of kids who fell between the cracks," he says. "If you were very bright, very athletic, very attractive, Parkland was great. But if you were one of those 'other' kids, it was easy to get lost."

Andy Roth became one of those "other" kids when he stopped playing football. With social groups tied to activities—sports, theater, music, art, science clubs—leaving an activity meant losing your place in the social order. For a teenager, it came close to losing your identity. Andy had played football with Owen since childhood, but an injury ended his athletic career in high school. The fact that Andy also attended classes at vocational-technical school instead of college prep classes made leaving athletics even more difficult. The vo-tech kids often felt invisible in a school where traditional academics were prized. Once he was off the team, he lost friendships with boys he'd known since playing youth football in elementary school.

"The other kids stopped talking to me. It's like, if you leave the family, that's it. It was never like that with Owen. Every time he saw me in school, he'd always yell, 'Hey, Andy.'" He pauses and adds, "It meant the world to me."

Owen's parents—both United Church of Christ ministers—played a part in instilling a sense of kindness and compassion in their sons. Both Kathy and Tom led by example. The congregation at Union United Church of Christ was defined by the gentleness that Tom displayed as its senior pastor. Visitors are quick to notice the friendly atmosphere, and Tom greeted newcomers by name by the time they had attended services three or four times. When the congregation voted to adopt the United Church of Christ's open and affirming congregation policy, welcoming people of all sexual orientations, gender identities, and gender expressions, Tom's presence helped to avoid a major rift. A former congregant, Gloria Ringer, says, "He had such an easy way with people. And a great memory for names and faces—and even for people's relatives." His sons displayed the same friendly, welcoming demeanor.

|||||||||||||

Jamie Berkowitz moved in social circles with some of the football boys' female friends, Kristen Dota and Irina Levin. A confident brunette with large, expressive blue eyes, Jamie drew Owen's attention at a party in winter 2006 during their junior year. Before long they were a couple. Like many teen romances, it was characterized by a series of breakups and reconciliations. During one breakup initiated by Jamie, Owen confided in Kristen Dota—one of the few people he allowed to see him cry.

Owen eventually stopped dating Jamie to return to his long-time crush, Abbie Benner. The idea of dating Abbie started when the boys were in preseason practice before their senior year. Mike Fay, already paired with Abbie's twin, Jess, encouraged Owen to join him to watch a favorite movie with the sisters. Romance blossomed from there.

Their relationship was an extension of the football boys' close-knit crowd. They spent all their time together, from school to the playing field to socializing at each other's houses. "We would be together all the time," Abbie says. "We would be together, but we could hang out with everyone else at the same time. Our circle of friends was so close. We could just be together and be with our friends."

In the crisp fall days of senior year, it was easy to believe that football always would be at the center of their lives. Classes and the prom, romances and academic honors—all the other things that marked that final year of high school were incidental to the experience of that last season as Parkland Trojans.

For Owen and his friends, it was a time measured by moments on a field, playing as part of an undefeated team, only the third one in Parkland history. There would be ten victories in regular season play. Six of them would be shutouts in which Parkland racked up scores as high as 49 and 54. Such a season lifts the powerful, shared experience of football into something nearly transcendent. Neuroscientist and Trinity College Dublin professor Ian H. Robertson describes it in his book *The Winner Effect: The Neuroscience of Success and Failure*. Robertson writes that winning makes you more confident and focused, which leads to more and greater victories. More importantly, it actually alters the chemistry of the brain. Winning increases testosterone, Robertson writes, which in turn increases the chemical messenger dopamine. When dopamine hits the reward network in the brain, it makes us feel better. It also makes winning addictive.

Little wonder that their senior season—an extraordinarily successful season until their loss in the District XI playoff game—would forever take on heightened importance in their lives. It became a memory wrapped in velvet, like a medal won in wartime, to be taken out and shined from time to time.

Some new rituals and traditions were added that fall. Spirits were high on bus rides returning home from away games. Players, tired but happy, beamed after the night's victory. In contrast to their youthful smiles, eye black smeared on their faces to reduce glare gave some the look of ancient warriors. Jamie Pagliaro strode down the center aisle of the bus, raising an index finger to silently proclaim "We're number one."

Owen, a knit cap pulled over his mane of flaming red hair, sat with a benevolent half-smile on his face as the team bus began its journey home. As the bus made its way up Cedar Crest Boulevard toward the high school, it passed over a bridge, the signal for him to spring into action. Hitting the side of the metal bus with the flat of his hand, he would yell, "Thundercats!" As

Owen beat his hand against metal, the rest of the team took up the cheer, making the ensuing ruckus deafening. It happened on every ride home in fall 2006.

The boys knew that their days playing together would soon be over. The thought had been an abstraction, one that didn't seem real as long as they were still lifting together in the weight room and hanging out most evenings and weekends. For a time, some of them considered going to the same college, nursing the fantasy that they could continue to play football together.

"We were all recruited by Lafayette [College]," says Marc. "Owen, me, and Fay. We walked around campus talking about how cool it would be if we all went there together."

They were invited to a camp on a Saturday at Lafayette as part of the recruitment process. Mike and Owen had partied the night before, crashing at a friend's house. When Mike awakened in the darkened basement of the friend's house, long after the sun was up, he discovered Owen had left without him, later saying he didn't know where to find Mike. When Mike complained about being left behind, Owen told him, "You need to be responsible for yourself." Mike remembers, "He was driven and laser-focused—sometimes to a fault."

| | | | | | | | | | | | |

Earlier generations of athletes relived their best plays and proudest moments by reviewing record books and sharing memories. But for Owen and his friends, there was a more indelible record: the season highlights video. Such videos have become a staple for youth playing football. Young players who grew up watching their pro football heroes on the documentaries produced by the award-winning company NFL Films fantasized about seeing their own touchdowns immortalized, complete with music and voiceover narration. Players aspiring to play at Division I schools needed individual videos to help sell them to prospective coaches. Formerly, athletic talent could only be observed by scouts on recruiting visits, at football camps, and at combines; now it can be cued up and reviewed on demand, even watched on a cell phone.

Highlights videos—whether for individual athletes or teams—are part of the $15 billion annual youth sports industry. Today individual athletes can pay from $400 to well over $1,200 for videos sent to college scouts.[3] Costs have skyrocketed since the years when Owen and his friends played—but even in 2006, athletes and parents expected a well-produced video with voice-overs, music, and athlete interviews edited into the final product.

Parkland High School, like hundreds of other high schools, contracts to have a season video produced. When the boys were seniors, that video was made by Schaf's Video Productions, a company in Allentown specializing in capturing athletic memories for players and their families. The 2006 Trojans highlights video begins with narration in a woman's cultured voice, speaking in an English accent reminiscent of those heard on public television's *Masterpiece Theatre*.[4]

> There is a legend over twenty-eight centuries old of a city that was home of the world's greatest army. Alongside mortal men, the gods Apollo and Poseidon built the city of Troy. With the help of Aries, the god of war, the walls of the city remained unbreached.

On the video, images from paintings of ancient armies in conflict dissolve to the image of the helmets of the Parkland Trojans, held in the air by players huddled in a circle, as the narrator continues.

> Much like those ancient warriors, we can find the modern-day Trojans defending their gates against any savagery.

A montage of plays opens the film, awakening muscle memory for the players watching it. Successful interceptions.

Completed passes. Tie-breaking touchdowns. Bone-crushing hits receive special attention, celebrated as game-changing moments or chances to even the score. Slow motion transforms the hits into a kind of ballet combining grace and power. Years later, as the young men watch, their bodies unconsciously prepare for the next play. They lean forward as their senior season flickers across the screen. The video chronicles a victorious season, celebrating the kinds of games that are part of the lore of high school football—grudge matches and traditional rivalries.

Parkland's face-off against the Bethlehem Catholic High School Hawks—Becahi, as the school is referred to in the Lehigh Valley—was a classic grudge match. Owen talks about it in an interview in the video. He sits in a director's chair, his hair a silky cascade. A single word—Warriors—is visible on the front of his T-shirt.

"We just hate them," he declares. "We just have a born hatred for Beca." His tone is matter-of-fact, belying the harshness of his words. "They rubbed it in our faces the year before, so we knew we had to take it to them. Some of the coaches got real emotional before the game."

He pauses, then continues in the same even tone, the softness of his voice contrasting with his threatening words. It surprises no one: This is football, a game built on crushing hits and domination.

"We just came in and punched them. We kicked them right in the face. It's something that we needed to do. It got our season off to a great start. It's something that propelled us into the rest of the season."

On the video, the victory against Becahi unspools from the opening kickoff. Play after play, the Trojans stop the Hawks and put points on the scoreboard. Coach Morgans, clad in one of the red polo shirts worn by Parkland's coaching staff, leans forward, intent, watching the action. A touchdown by Greg Bortz in the first quarter starts the rout, with two more touchdowns to follow. "The Trojans are unstoppable," the play-by-play announcer intones. By halftime the score is 21–0. It's Owen who scores the final touchdown. Stepping out of a tackle amid a swarm of Beca players in black and gold, he gives an almost balletic hop before he takes it into the end zone to bring Parkland to its winning score of 35–0.

The highlights reel ends with Parkland's traditional rivalry against the Zephyrs of Whitehall High School. Each year the two teams play for bragging rights and to claim the Gerencser Trophy, named for a coach who had a hand in establishing a winning football program at both schools. Joe Gerencser, a legendary coach who successfully led the Trojans for fourteen seasons, is credited with building the school's football program after he arrived in 1962. In those days, other schools referred to Parkland's team as the Farmers, reflecting a time a half-century ago when the district had far more farmland than suburban sprawl. Before Gerencser left Parkland after the 1976 season, he had compiled a record of 97–36–7, with two undefeated seasons. He finished his career as the head coach at Whitehall for eleven years, retiring in 1986. A tough coach known for having little tolerance for bull from his players or his coaching staff, he was honored in 1995 shortly before his death from cancer with a perpetual trophy created in his name. In 2006, the teams met in the last game of the season, bringing an undefeated Parkland against a Whitehall team with a 5–4 record heading into the game. The Trojans trounced the Zephyrs, 28–13.

Players about to play their last games as Trojans are further recognized in a rite of passage known as Senior Night, held during the last home game of the season. Each senior walks the fifty-yard line with their parents as a wistful reminder that their high school days on the gridiron are ending. A light rain fell before the game on October 27 as senior players lined up with their parents, waiting to be recognized. Some mothers popped golf umbrellas as they prepared to make the walk with their sons. Each walk reflected that player's relationship with his parents and provided a glimpse into his family life. Some were joined by a single parent. Number 28, Erik Rueda, strode out, his mother's arm hooked through his. Hesham Abdelaal, number 71, carried his helmet over his arm. He turned to his mother and smiled before they walked together across the field. Dan Boyko balanced a younger sibling on his hip—clearly a move he'd often practiced—as he and his mother marched across.

Others were accompanied by both parents. Marc Quilling, wearing number 15, stepped up, flanked by his parents, helmet in hand. He paused as his name was called, bent and kissed his mother, and walked confidently on to the turf.

Next came Owen, Samson-like red hair cascading on his shoulders, stepping up with his father—almost the same height—on his right. Tom, an umbrella tucked under his arm, wore a Parkland sweatshirt. Owen's mother, dwarfed by her husband and son, was on Owen's left. Kathy wore a red jacket, a large mum corsage pinned on its lapel with a *P* for Parkland in the center. Owen looked down at her with affection, throwing one arm around her shoulders and the other around his father. The threesome walked across the field as a single unit. Next came Mike Fay, wearing number 75 and flanked by his parents, now divorced. Mike spent hours at Owen's house, playing video games, riding out his parents' breakup. On the field at Senior Night, he was a buffer between them, walking in the middle and holding his mother's hand. Stepping up next, number 90, Jamie Pagliaro, ducked his head to give his mother a quick kiss before stepping out with his parents. His boyish face lacked the chiseled angularity of manhood that will come with maturity.

With the ritual of Senior Night behind them and that night's win recorded in the record books, the football boys looked ahead to postseason play. In less than a week, it would be November. In less than a week, the team would beat East Stroudsburg's Cavaliers 21–7 in the first round of postseason play. And then they would face Easton's Red Rovers in the Pennsylvania Interscholastic Athletic Association District 11 finals. For some members of the Trojans, it wouldn't be the first time they had faced Easton in a championship game. For some players, it would not be the first time Easton had beaten them. They had faced Easton in middle school under Coach Steckel and lost after an undefeated season. In both games, Owen delivered savage hits against Easton that his teammates will long remember. It would be the second time that, in spite of those hits, they lost the game.

Marc Quilling would remember it all. When the Parkland Trojan Alumni Varsity Club sold engraved bricks years later to form a path near the high school athletics entrance, Marc bought one. "RIP OT #31" is etched into his brick's red surface, a nod to Owen's jersey number. Below that are the words "Thundercats! Football '06."

CHAPTER 7

PENN PALS

FOOTBALL RECRUITS AT the University of Pennsylvania were invited to a dinner on campus in the spring of their senior year in high school. The room buzzed with male voices, the voices of young men between the ages of eighteen and twenty-three forming an auditory collage of friends greeting friends, locker-room-like bantering and introductions of guys who would be joining the team in fall 2007.

"Hey, man."

"How's it going?"

"This is Adam. He's that guy who made that incredible play I was telling you about."

"What position do you play?"

Coming into the crowded room to take his place among the newest Penn Quakers, Owen cut an unlikely profile, his shoulder-length hair giving him a wild-man image quite different from most of the other recruits. Luke DeLuca, clean-cut and coming out of a gap year spent at boarding school at Phillips Academy Andover in Massachusetts, sized up the guy who would become his roommate. Despite his long hair, Owen was as neatly dressed as the others in sport coat and tie. Except that the tie he wore had lobsters on it—a trademark piece of haberdashery that had been his favorite at high school football banquets. At that first dinner, Owen's hair and tie placed him in the category of "different." "People weren't sure what to think," Luke says.

His new teammates weren't the first to wonder if Owen would fit in at Penn. His parents were surprised when he chose to study business at the Wharton School because he had most often talked about studying engineering and playing football at Lehigh University near his home in the Lehigh Valley. The Lehigh coaches had recruited him.

"I don't know why he chose [Penn]," Tom says, speculating about his son's reasons. "He was never interested in finance, he just wanted to be the boss in charge. I think that's how he saw himself: 'If I study business, I could be the boss in charge.'"

Later, Owen would admit he also saw attending Penn as a way to make good at the school where his older brother Matt had failed, abandoning his athletic and academic careers before graduating.

"One time he said to me that he felt the pressure to undo Matt screwing up," Tom recalls. "He put the pressure on himself. I don't know why he felt that."

His friends also wondered about his choice.

Attending a business school where graduates tended to focus on the accrual of wealth seemed an especially odd match. Although he had an innate ability to get along with people from many social and economic groups, wealth and status meant little to him. Mike Fay, whose older brother Joey had graduated from Wharton, pondered the contrast between the school's culture and his friend's persona. "I often thought, 'Here's Owen, going to business school. He wears hand-me-down clothes and shoes with holes in them. He drives a Chevy Lumina. And he's just the salt of the earth. He walks around like he's wearing a Versace suit,'" Mike said.

Yet Fay and other Parkland classmates never wondered if their friend could handle the academic demands of the Ivy League. "He was a natural," Mike said.

||||||||||||

With the start of football camp in August, Owen and Luke moved into a campus complex known as the Quad, short for the Quadrangle. The original structure, built in 1895, grouped brick buildings around courtyards in a style that had come to characterize college architecture. Made up of three separate college houses that encompassed thirty-nine individual houses, it was where many Penn freshman lived. Owen and Luke were in Fisher Hassenfeld College House. Getting to know the guy he'd glimpsed at the spring dinner for recruits, Luke learned Owen was as different as his appearance suggested. "He was his own person," Luke said. "He didn't care what anyone thought about him."

Football was their common ground. Luke had come to the sport much later than Owen and the Parkland boys, most of whom had started playing in elementary school. He began playing as a middle schooler in Grand Island, New York, a community near Buffalo often impacted by subzero temperatures and lake effect snow. Although his father and uncle had both played football, it was not their example that drew him: Luke started playing because many of his friends did. He continued when he entered high school at St. Joseph's Collegiate Institute in nearby Buffalo. The opportunity to extend his high school career and play at Phillips Andover had come from a St. Joseph's alumnus with ties to the prep school. He and Owen shared the experience of playing both ways—offense and defense—on their high school teams.

As roommates, they quickly fell into an easy camaraderie built around the routine of being college football players: practices, weight lifting, team breakfasts before Saturday games, required study halls during the week. At night, they kept their room freezing, setting the air conditioner to what they called the "double snowflake," regardless of the weather outside. Friends who crashed in their room for the night rarely returned because of its meat locker frigidity. The roommates loved it. They also loved joining a football program steeped in tradition. Penn was the alma mater of John Heisman, for whom the prestigious Heisman Trophy, awarded to the most outstanding player in NCAA football, is named. Franklin Field, where the Quakers played, is acknowledged as the oldest stadium still operating for football games. Originally opened in 1895 and rebuilt in 1922, the stadium boasts a history that includes being the site of the fabled Army-Navy game, the site of Vince Lombardi's only NFL playoff loss in 1960, and the site of the first radio broadcast and television telecast of football games. For good measure, it was the Philadelphia Eagles' home field for thirteen years.[1] For young men who had grown up with football occupying a central role in their lives, playing there was like becoming part of the game's history.

|||||||||||||

Jake Peterson returned to Penn in 2007, the same year that Owen entered the university. A member of the Church of Jesus Christ of Latter Day Saints, he'd taken time off to serve on a mission, a typical practice among young Mormons. Upon his return, he immediately gravitated to the freshman with the mane of red hair. "First time I saw him, I looked at his super long, gorgeous hair and thought, 'Nice: there's someone else,'" said Peterson, who'd been known for his long, blond locks during his first year at Penn. He had to cut them short to serve as a missionary. Now, back on campus and growing out his trademark hair, he'd returned to playing football for the Quakers.

Jake's father, Clay, played football at Brigham Young University in the years when Jim McMahon played quarterback before beginning his fifteen-year NFL career that included playing on the Chicago Bears and Green Bay Packers Super Bowl championship teams. "My dad went to the coach and asked, 'Where do you need me?' and the coach said, 'We could use more people on the defensive line,'" Jake says, savoring the piece of family football lore. "So he bulked up to 285 and played defensive end."

It was a given that Jake, Clay's firstborn, would play football. "From the time I was a week old, he would hold me and whisper, 'Jake you're going to be a linebacker,'" Jake said. While some youngsters slept with stuffed animals, Jake slept with a toy football. He started playing in elementary school, joining a Pop Warner team at around age ten. "I was a linebacker from the time I stepped on the field," he says, noting that he also played defensive end in high school.

As an inside linebacker at Penn, Peterson wore number 39, and had a locker next to number 40—Owen Thomas. Times in the locker room were a nonstop comedy routine because of the repartee between Owen and Justin Cosgrove, who wore number 38 and had the adjacent locker. Adam Triglia, another pal, was always ready to chime in. Owen, Justin, and Adam would become housemates as sophomores.

As lockers clanged and teammates donned pads and uniforms, the banter often took the form of heated debate, with Justin and Owen arguing about issues that could never be resolved. Whether the '72 Celtics could have beaten the Knicks. Whether Justin or Owen could lay claim to being best at playing *Call of Duty*. About things of zero consequence to anyone except the members of this football brotherhood on a particular Saturday morning in fall. At some point, Adam would chime in with his heavy New York accent. "I told them all the time they needed to have their own TV show," Jake said.

In practices and on the field, Jake found his match in Owen. Both were aggressive players who always brought a high level of focus and energy to practices. They frequently paired up on pass rush drills, growling like two bears as they approached one another, each bringing an intensity that surpassed many of their teammates. Jake admired Owen's ability to play aggressively without becoming negative or nasty. "He had that ability to lift people up all the time," he says. "One thing I struggled with was anger management. I was mean. Unfortunately for me, I'd become very negative on the field."

His anger had been encouraged throughout his playing career. Jake's high school coaches had encouraged his highly aggressive style in his hometown of Lake Tahoe, Nevada. "During playing, I knocked out multiple players. I deliberately targeted head-to-head contact. I don't think my mental state was very healthy. In my mind that's what made sense," he says. Over the years, some coaches would pay him five- and ten-dollar bonuses for heavy hits delivered in practice.

Jake worked to balance his negativity with his commitment to his religious faith. A strong belief in Christ was something else he had in common with his redheaded teammate. Sometimes the two young men lingered in the locker room after practice long after others had gone, praying together for guidance. Jake was allowed to see a persona that seldom surfaced among Owen's other friends: the son of ministers who had a deep commitment to his Christian faith.

"Most college guys on a football team don't focus on that," Jake said. "With him and me, we'd talk a lot about that. . . . He had a very good understanding of the Gospel, probably because his parents are ministers. We were able to talk about some deeper things that some people didn't have the frame of reference to discuss."

||||||||||||||

Owen and his freshman-year roommate, Luke DeLuca, moved to what they would call "the Baltimore house" in fall 2008, at the start of their sophomore year. The rowhouses on the 3900 block of Baltimore Avenue in Philadelphia stand shoulder to shoulder, like solid redbrick linemen on a football team. The neighborhood is favored by Penn athletes living off campus. It's a short sprint down 39th Street from the university's fabled

Locust Walk. It's a bit more of a jog—more than a mile—from legendary Franklin Field, where the Quakers play football, which makes it a good stretch of the legs for players shuttling back and forth for games and practices.

The house on Baltimore Avenue was a legacy residence for Penn football players, passed down after every graduation. As one group of senior players vacated the row house, a group of underclassmen inherited it. It was one of several acknowledged among students to be a "football house," where group after group of Quakers teammates made their home. It was one of several football houses dotting the neighborhood. Jake Peterson and some of his friends on the team lived a few doors away, and other teammates lived nearby.

Owen and Luke were joined in the house by three of their sophomore teammates who had also lived in their campus dorm—Adam Triglia, Justin Cosgrove, and Kale Farley. Farley, a carefree guy from Texas, didn't survive Penn's academic rigor. By summer 2009, he had left the university, his spot in the house filled by Dave Macknet. Macknet had transferred to Penn the year before.

Luke remembers the place with nostalgia. "That was a really cool house over there. That was the house where everything happened," he said.

Each of the guys had his own room, with Luke and Adam on the first floor, and Owen, Justin, and Kale—followed by Dave—on the second floor. On the third floor was the shared living space, with a common living room, kitchen, and outdoor balcony. If the house had a decorating scheme, it was clutter, with coordinating grime and vermin.

Owen's father, Tom, would walk into the vestibule and tread on a thick carpet of unopened mail whenever he came to visit. "No one ever touched the mail," he said. Trash was disposed of by dropping bags from the third-floor balcony and watching them explode in the alley space between the row houses. Such practices encouraged an influx of mice and cockroaches, already a challenge in city neighborhoods. They weren't the only critters to pay a visit. Once, sitting on the balcony overlooking the garbage-strewn scene below, Owen had found himself face-to-face with a large raccoon foraging for scraps. The girlfriends and female acquaintances of the house's inhabitants had one word to describe the atmosphere: disgusting.

Owen and Abbie Benner, who was then attending Millersville University eighty miles away in Lancaster County, had continued their relationship after going to college. She frequently visited him and stayed in the apartment, cringing at the sound of the mice. "In the middle of the night, you could hear them chewing on paper, and you could hear the mousetraps going off," Abbie said, shuddering.

Walking through the kitchen, visitors picked their way through a path of upended paper cups used to trap cockroaches. "We wouldn't kill them because, when you kill them, they let out a pheromone and that would bring all their friends," Luke explained. "So we would just put a cup over them in the kitchen."

Although the five inhabitants sometimes made an attempt to clean when female guests visited, for the most part they relished their trashed living conditions. "We all just loved that we didn't have to worry about anything," Luke said.

Socializing, not studying, was the focus for the five roommates. "I don't think I once studied successfully in that house," said Dave, who went on to Robert Wood Johnson Medical School at Rutgers University and then to an orthopedic surgery residency. "I skipped a lot of classes just to hang out with those guys."

Luke concurred. "I would find myself doing all-nighters. I would not be able to do work when everyone was awake; I wanted to be hanging out with them. Sometimes I'd have to go to the library to get away from everyone."

In the living room, two television sets provided a focal point. The larger one was for watching movies with the smaller one reserved for video games. A small chair was positioned for the video game player to sit. Guys waiting to take their turn lounged behind it on a red couch. The young men spent hours rotating on and off the sofa, taking their place at the game controls. As Owen took his turn playing his favorite game, *Call of Duty*, the air was filled with sound effects. Lobbing virtual grenades on foes, his mouth opened wide to mimic the sound of explosions. Seven hits entitled him to send in dogs to aid in the attack. "Send in the digs," he screamed, giving a classic Owen twist to the word for a canine.

Procrastination—a venerable pastime for college students—was raised to high art by the five inhabitants of the football house. The video games and ready access to a group of best friends for nonstop talk were favored ways to avoid the inevitable demands of academics. In addition to the shared distractions, each of the men had his own way to kill time.

Owen frequently rearranged the furniture in his room while listening to his favorite music—Led Zeppelin, Incubus, and Third Eye Blind. The sound of the Led Zeppelin hit "Over the Hills and Far Away" signaled that Owen was up and about. A visit to his room would reveal a new floor plan. Desk, bed, and bookcases would all be rotated.

Classes might be cut and homework postponed, but there was no procrastination when it came to the game of football. The young men seldom deviated from the regimented schedule of lifting and conditioning, practices, and watching film. The commitment went beyond the threat of being cut from the team. It was a discipline that they embraced for love of the game. Owen retained a level of enthusiasm for workouts that was matched by few.

On an early morning in late fall, Jake Peterson trudged down Baltimore Avenue, a cloud of foggy breath floating above his face in the cold. He didn't mind getting up early, but—a true West Coast native—Jake hated the cold. His dislike was reflected in everything about him: the layers of clothes he wore, his unhappy expression, and his loud grumbling that he wished he were running on an indoor heated track.

As other football players gathered from nearby football houses for their run, Jake did a double take. There was Owen Thomas, unbelievably wearing shorts and a cut-off T-shirt despite the frigid temperatures. And he would be singing. Singing! Typically it might be a tune by Third Eye Blind or Incubus. Heavy metal was usually reserved for the weight room or game day. Jake shook his head and broke into a grin in spite of himself.

Soon a group of Penn players had assembled to start their mandatory run. For a few minutes everyone would be quiet as their feet hit macadam, their heavy breathing and grunts so low that the sound was almost subliminal. Suddenly, Owen would speak, his nonstop patter a counterpoint to the sounds of physical exertion

"Gentlemen, we got to yoke the youlders," he shouted. It would take the runners a minute to process it. Youlders . . . Owen's offbeat lingo. And pretty soon the whole crowd of tough football players was laughing together and talking about shoulders.

"From the very start, all the way, he just had that effect on people," Jake said. "It's hard to be upset when you're laughing."

In the Penn weight room, Owen recaptured some of the atmosphere that he had created during high school. Clad in a raggedy T-shirt, hair topped by a bandana—"He looked like a homeless person," Jake Peterson quipped—he would crank up the music, playing heavy metal and classic rock while he lifted. Jim Steel, Penn's strength and conditioning manager, shared Owen's love of the classic tunes and enjoyed hearing the music played at a high decibel.

Owen's offbeat way of talking made its way from workouts to practice field to the playing field at Penn, permeating the football team, just as it had done in high school. His invented words soon became an accepted part of the Penn football program, even making their way into team meetings. "He'd say something using that lingo, completely serious, to the coaches and the coach would know exactly what he meant. Everyone would burst out laughing," Luke said.

Even his trash talk on the field, meant to disarm opponents, included language that was quintessentially Owen. Facing his opponents across the line, he kept up a barrage of nonstop jabber, which at first sounded nonsensical to players on the other team.

"I'm coming at you like a puma cat."

"I've been eating vegetables all week like a deer."

"Are you ready for the lonely satchel? 'Cause I'm bringing it."

And while the other players were trying to figure out what to make of the big guy who sounded like he was saying a bunch of ominous nonsense, Owen would be getting ready to take them out of the game.

"Sometimes," Jake recalled, "he'd been making sound effects, like explosions, as he was running through these guys."

｜｜｜｜｜｜｜｜｜｜｜｜｜

The Penn locker room was full of big personalities when Daniel Lipschutz entered it as a freshman place kicker and punter in fall 2008, when Owen was a sophomore. A quiet guy from Ambler, Pennsylvania, in nearby Montgomery County, not far from Penn's campus, Daniel had started playing football in high school after growing up playing soccer. "I'd felt I'd maxed out my potential in soccer," he recalls. As a teen who was shy and lacked self-assurance, changing to football had benefits. "When I switched to playing football. . . . It brought me into my own. When you're fifteen, sixteen years old, people start to see themselves differently. The football mind-set is such a masculine environment. It brought out my personality. What football gave me in high school and moving on into college—it gave me such an identity. I think that helped me to maneuver socially and culturally."

It was another example of the brotherhood that the football team offered to members. The identity of football player traveled with young men from high school to college, easing the transition. The brotherhood's culture was almost tribal in nature, linked by shared goals, traditions, and rituals. In the tribe that was Penn football, Owen emerged as a leader.

"Anyone who walked in—it could have been the president of the university, it could have been his mom, his dad—he would have a big reaction, as if they were the most important person who had shown up that day," Daniel recalled, describing Owen's typical manner of greeting people. "And that's just really true, the genuine feeling that you were a special person to him and that every moment was one to be sort of celebrated. That's the kind of feeling that he left everybody with."

Owen's positive presence was a plus for players working under a coach known for being tough. "You might say we survived playing football together under Al Bagnoli," Daniel says wryly. Bagnoli had a no-nonsense approach that led to success. Considered one of the most successful coaches in the Ivy League, he coached at Penn for twenty-three years. During that time, he amassed nine Ivy League championships, six undefeated seasons, and three perfect seasons. One of the Ivy League championships would be won in Owen Thomas's last season. The season following his death, the Quakers would win a second title.[2]

Compliments could be hard to come by on Bagnoli's teams.

Even after a good practice or winning a game in which they had dominated the other team, the Quakers would find "Bags," as they called the coach behind his back, cursing and critical, focusing on weaknesses in their performance. He rarely gave compliments. "The best thing Bagnoli ever said to me after a play was, 'That wasn't as bad as I thought it was going to be,'" Daniel said.

Owen acted as a buffer between the coach and his team-mates, and his ability to rally the team would lead to his election as team captain in spring 2010, days before his death.

"He was someone who would take the younger kids under his wing and really capture their interest," Dave Macknet said. "He would show them his passion for the game and for the team and for Penn. And you can't help but follow that passion."

On the field, Owen continued to be the powerful presence he had been for most of his life, displaying the hard-hitting style that was his trademark. As part of Penn's kickoff return team, he was the center of the wedge, the group of players that forms a vicious, high-speed shield for the player returning the kickoff. The NCAA would ban the wedge block formation in April 2010, less than two weeks before Owen would die by suicide. NCAA studies showed that 20 percent of all injuries on kickoffs resulted in concussions, lending the impetus for banning a formation that promoted forceful hits. The NFL had banned it the previous year. The introduction of the wedge formation—earlier called the "flying wedge"—happened in an 1892 game between Harvard and Yale. Rules outlawing the wedge and its often brutal outcome were introduced as early as 1894. Eventually, forward motion would be outlawed behind the line of scrimmage to keep the offense from getting a full-steam-ahead running start.[3] But lovers of the game acknowledge that it was the ultimate play for testing the mettle of players on kickoffs. It was the singular weapon among players on special teams.

Owen had initially been frustrated about seeing little play as a freshman, but by his sophomore year, he was starting on defense. What was already nearly a decade of achievement in football would continue in college. As a sophomore, he started in all ten games as a defensive end, making ten tackles on the season—six solo. As a junior, he was once again a standout, earning All-Ivy second team honors, playing on a team that won the Ivy League championship. He led the team and finished second in the Ivy League with six sacks and had a season best eight tackles in the Quakers' win over Bucknell. Owen was making a name for himself on the field. The website Bleacher-Report.com would single him out as one of the top Ivy League football players of 2010 on the defensive line.[4]

CHAPTER 8

FOOTBALL FAMILY

IN HER HIGH SCHOOL AND COLLEGE YEARS, Boston University researcher Dr. Ann McKee would easily have fit in among the friends who congregated at the Baltimore house with Owen and his Penn football brothers. Like most of those young men, she'd grown up in a football family in her hometown of Appleton, Wisconsin. The youngest among five children, she remembers joining her brothers for football drills and running tires set up by the high school football coach who was a family friend. Her father had played football at Grinnell College. Her older brother Chuck, seven years her senior, was a star player at Appleton East High School, where McKee later was a cheerleader—then the accepted option for a girl. As a kid, her pride in her brother's gridiron prowess prompted her to mount signs on the family front lawn boasting, "Chuck McKee Lives Here." Chuck later would play quarterback at Division III Lawrence University in their hometown, eschewing Division I offers to focus on academics. As a Wisconsin native, McKee was a "cheesehead" by birthright and embraced the title as a fan of the Green Bay Packers from childhood. In adulthood, she had her own cheesehead hat, shaped like a giant wedge of cheese, to prove it.[1]

By the time she entered the University of Wisconsin at eighteen, she'd developed a love of art equal to her love of football.

Painting was her passion. "But I quickly realized I wasn't going to be able to support myself," McKee says. "You know, I could be an art teacher. I had limited options." Once again inspired by her brother Chuck, who by then was a doctor, she switched her major from art to science with an eye on a medical career. It wasn't an easy choice. McKee had focused on English, languages, and the liberal arts during high school. "I just did a lot of extra work that first year," she says, matter-of-factly describing the way she scrambled to catch up with college classmates who had focused on the sciences. It reflected a singular determination that would manifest itself again when she became a medical researcher pursuing elusive answers in the lab.

After completing medical school at Case Western Reserve Medical School in Cleveland, she initially specialized in internal medicine, but sometime during her residency at Cleveland Metropolitan General Hospital, McKee fell in love with studying and treating the brain. Her specialty became neurology.[2] She eventually switched to neuropathology, a focus that surprised no one who knew her penchant for art. It is a highly visual field, a specialty in which McKee studies the patterns of proteins and abnormalities in the brain.[3] Only an artist turned scientist like McKee would gaze at a specimen under her microscope and proclaim that it showed a "beautiful pathology."

Her first experiences with studying tau protein were in the brains of Alzheimer's patients, first as director of Boston University's Alzheimer's Disease Center and then as director of brain banks for the Framingham Heart Study and the Centenarian Study. It was while she was in those roles that she had happened upon the cases of two former boxers, one in 2003 and a second in 2005, who had initially been diagnosed with Alzheimer's. Both exhibited a buildup of tau protein quite unlike what was found in that disease. Hearing about the intriguing case of former Pittsburgh Steeler Mike Webster by a then-unknown doctor, Bennet Omalu, piqued her interest still more. Omalu named the new disease chronic traumatic encephalopathy, or CTE. It was marked by the same kind of buildup of tau McKee had seen in the boxers.[4] What was going on in the brains of those old fighters, that NFL superstar, she wondered? Her scientific curiosity and her reputation as a researcher would land her squarely in the middle of the hunt to find an answer.

In 2008, when Owen Thomas and his friends were sophomores headed for their junior year at Penn, McKee became the director of Boston University's Center for the Study of Traumatic Encephalopathy. She'd been suggested for the job by Dr. Robert Stern, a Boston University professor of neurology and neurosurgery who had worked with her on the university's Alzheimer's disease research. In forming the center, its cofounders—Chris Nowinski, PhD, and Dr. Robert Cantu—had parted ways with Dr. Bennet Omalu, deeming him too difficult a collaborator. They needed another researcher for their center, and McKee was the choice. Nowinski began to collect the brains of former athletes for her research at the center. On the surface, the work of gathering brains sounded ghoulish, like a bad horror movie. But finding donors who agreed to give their brains after death to study CTE was critical to advancing research and advocacy efforts. Without collecting the brains of former athletes, research about the disease would advance only glacially.

The first brain he got her was that of John Grimsley, an ex-linebacker for the Houston Oilers. McKee found his brain was riddled with CTE—a discovery that astonished her and sent her flying to share the news with her brother Chuck, the former football player. That case, and the ones that followed, confirmed a pattern: men who played football and suffered jarring hits and concussions were getting a debilitating neurodegenerative disease that was changing their personalities, destroying memory, spawning impulsivity, sending some into spiraling depression, and leading to early death.[5]

McKee's first public appearance as the face of CTE research was at the press conference Nowinski staged at the 2009 Super

Bowl. There, she announced that CTE had been found in the brain of Tom McHale, a former Tampa Bay Buccaneer who played nine years in the NFL. McHale was only forty-five at the time of his death, she told reporters, but he had a brain like that of an elderly boxer. The announcement caused barely a ripple, swallowed up by the hoopla of the Super Bowl. But Nowinski, McKee, and company would soon be called to meet with the NFL.[6]

The NFL and its representatives were slow, even dilatory, about giving credence to the research about CTE. If you ask McKee, she'd say the organization had been especially sluggish about according credibility to a woman. It was widely reported that she felt the league was "dismissive" of her work at a pre-dominately male meeting held at league headquarters on May 19, 2009, that included Nowinski and Daniel Perl, director of the US Department of Defense's Center for Neuroscience and Regenerative Medicine, where the focus is on brain trauma among combat veterans.[7]

In those early days of CTE research, McKee kept two facets of her life in precarious balance. Her lifelong love of football and her research into the damaged brains of former football players coexisted. She still felt a strong affinity for the game that was part of her family—so much so that she was disappointed when her only son, Graham, chose to play soccer over football. Her respect for the sport and the athletes who played it helped to fuel her determination to find answers about the brain trauma found in some of its stars. But on Sundays, she still watched the Green Bay Packers, still kept a bobblehead of Packers quarterback Brett Favre in her office.[8]

||||||||||||||

Although Owen continued to excel athletically, the academic success that he had achieved at Parkland High School often eluded him at Penn. What once had come easily now required significantly greater effort. Many in Parkland actually had grade point averages higher than 4.0 because grades earned in Advanced Placement and honors classes were "weighted," carrying more points when calculating averages, to signify it was a more difficult class. It was a practice adopted by many school districts catering to a generation known as millennials who researchers have characterized as feeling a sense of entitlement.[9] Acknowledged and rewarded just for showing up during their formative years—when earning awards for participation instead of achievement became standard—the generation supported a system that awarded them special grades for doing more difficult work. It was a system that could also lead to disappointment.

An Ivy League school like Penn is filled with students who were academic superstars in high school. Like Owen, Jake Peterson experienced the letdown of being just another good student among many. "To be honest, it was hard for me at Penn, to come in and always have been the top student. Then you come in, and everyone's smarter," Jake said. He noted that students not involved in athletics would have additional hours to study.

Like Jake, Owen struggled when he entered college. When his high school friends compared notes about their first semesters at their respective schools, they remembered he complained about a math class. "I just can't get it," Owen said. It was a surprising statement from the friend they considered the most academically gifted in their crowd. His father, given permission to access Owen's account for financial aid paperwork, saw that the former straight-A student had earned a D in calculus.

A supportive girlfriend, Abbie would help him to study, making him flash cards and quizzing him before tests. He pulled all-nighters and still failed to earn the top grades he'd earned in high school.

Jake said that the Wharton School—legendary for a high-pressured, cutthroat culture among its students—was exceptionally tough, even in the already challenging academic atmosphere that pervaded Penn.

"There's a lot of guys who play football who go through Wharton. Not any of them do real great," Jake said candidly, adding that the general atmosphere in the business school made it even more difficult. "Everyone's out to get each other. It ends up being a very negative environment." Owen, who, perhaps because of his athletic background, was the epitome of a team player, did not relate well to the "take no prisoners" attitude of his business school classmates. He was competitive but tended to focus on contributing as part of a team. In addition to his own achievement, he also wanted others to succeed.

|||||||||||||

Adam Grant came to the University of Pennsylvania in 2009 and in a short time became a superstar professor, consistently earning recognition as a top teacher at the university while winning international acclaim as an influential management thinker. By 2013, he'd published *The New York Times* bestseller *Give and Take*, which examines why helping others drives personal success. He later would write two more best-selling books, *Originals* and *Option B*, coauthored with Sheryl Sandberg, chief operating officer at Facebook. The latter book, published in 2017, would examine facing adversity and building resilience. Much of Sandberg's portion of the book would focus on the sudden loss of her husband, Dave Goldberg, CEO of SurveyMonkey. At the beginning of chapter 3, Grant would recall the unique classroom contributions and the untimely death of his student Owen Thomas.

"There are students who make a mark and who change you in ways that you didn't expect. . . . I can't think of a student who's done that more than Owen," Grant said. During Grant's first term teaching at Wharton in fall 2009, Owen was in his Organizational Behavior class. A formidable physical presence at over two hundred pounds, his red hair an exclamation point on top of his head, Owen bounded into Grant's classroom and claimed a seat in the front row. It was the seat he would occupy for the rest of the semester, tossing insightful questions into discussions as effortlessly as he fired footballs at practice.

"I think it was sort of emblematic of who Owen was. He was larger than life," Grant recalled. "He was full of energy and joy and curiosity. You could see it all over his face and the way that he walked. This was somebody who loved life and loved sharing and soaking up all of the great things that the people around him had to offer."

It set him apart from other Wharton students. Grant acknowledged that undergraduate business students could become pressured to amass the right experiences on their resumes or to worry that a classmate might be competing with them for a prestigious, high-paying job or internship, or for top grades in a class. Owen was different.

"You know, Owen was a breath of fresh air in that environment, somebody who came in and said, 'I'm here to learn,'" Grant said.

Owen's attitude would earn him the accolade "The Most Cooperative Negotiator" in Grant's class, an anecdote recorded in *Option B*. In some ways it was a dubious honor in a course where students were required to do role plays negotiating deals. Most of the students would assume positions that were assertive, hard-nosed, and savvy. Not Owen.

"He sat down and he was there to help the other person achieve their goals, and then he was happy with whatever was leftover, and that was striking. It was unusual," Grant said. He paused before adding, "You know, everyone recognized it as unusual."

When Grant asked students to evaluate the class, he received surprising answers to the open-ended question "Any other comments about the class?" They wrote things like, "Yeah, I just want to comment that Owen Thomas is a highlight of being in this class and on this campus and . . . knowing him makes my life better." When asked, "What part of this class most enriched your life?," several answered, "Working on a project with Owen."

Grant was amazed at the feedback. "That was the answer that came up more than once, and it does not happen every day. It doesn't even happen in every class or every year or every decade, right?" Grant chuckled. "That stands out."

Later, writing *Give and Take*, Grant said he realized Owen had been the quintessential giver. "I felt like every person he met, his first goal was to figure out how he could help them and what he could add to their lives. And the remarkable thing was, he often added to their lives just by virtue of them knowing him," Grant said. "You meet Owen Thomas and, all of a sudden, you realize, 'Wow, there are some extraordinary human beings on the planet.'"

It was clear, in the campus culture some referred to as the Penn Bubble, Owen was recognized as he had been throughout his life—a charismatic figure who was genuine, fun-loving, and sincere. So it came as a surprise when he confided to Mike Fay, John Zaccaro, Jamie Pagliaro, and other high school friends that the pictures that they saw on Facebook and other forms of social media that showed him having a great time did not completely reflect how he felt. Mike and Jamie both recalled that he told them that he felt lonely in the city.

||||||||||||||

While embracing new academic and athletic experiences, Owen retained ties with what had been part of the most perfect and important part of his life—the time spent as a Parkland Trojan playing high school football. His continuing romantic involvement with Abbie helped him to straddle the old and the new, the life of a Penn student and that of a Parkland football boy. High school friends who attended college within driving distance of Philadelphia visited the house on Baltimore Avenue for parties. Emily Toth DeLuca met her future spouse, Owen's roommate Luke, on such a visit, while she was still dating her high school boyfriend. Abbie's sister Jess continued to date his hometown buddy Mike Fay, another Parkland connection.

At home, Owen's house remained a gathering place for the Parkland football boys. During one break, he invited his high school friends to a party, even though he still had a term paper to finish. Music blasted in the Thomases' basement rec room as friends walked in and out. Owen sat in the center of it all, laptop balanced in his lap, only occasionally looking up to admonish one of the guys: "Hey, don't break that."

Owen and his high school teammates realized soon after starting their college football careers that the game they loved as boys was now a different experience. High school football, while requiring commitment, was carefree when compared to the demands of playing in college. Their high school coach, Jim Morgans, had been a father figure. College coaches, whose jobs often hinge on win-loss records, tend to be all business. It is equally intense for college players, who live the game 24/7, rooming with teammates and planning class schedules around athletic commitments.

"You play in high school, and it's because of the friends, the camaraderie. You play in college and survive four years, it's because you love the game," said Marc Quilling. "In college, it's not an easy thing, when you've got a full academic load, you have six a.m. lifts, and go to three classes or whatever. Maybe you take a quick nap after lunch. Then you go right down to films, practice, dinner, study hall. Then you do it all over again. It's a full-time job. It's a double major. Because Saturdays and Sundays are full too. Saturday's a game day. Sunday you're waking up early. We do a full workout and we're watching films."

Despite the grueling schedule, Owen and Marc were forging close relationships and finding a new brotherhood at their colleges. Mike Fay was disappointed by the lack of commitment among his teammates at Kent State University in Ohio. With 120 players on the team, only a handful of starters, which included Mike, were committed to winning. The second and third string players huddled around heaters on the sidelines, oblivious to the play happening on the field.

"It was very apathetic, our school, towards football, Kent State. Not a very good tradition. No one really cared," Mike says. "We would go five wins, seven losses." At the end of the season his father would encourage him to stay, telling him to give it one more year. Before he knew it, one year turned into two, then three.

Jamie Pagliaro relished his college career playing for the Tribe at the College of William & Mary, but he sometimes felt the stress of balancing academics and athletics. "William & Mary was hard. Keeping up my grades was tough. And then you had football, with working out at six in the morning," Jamie said. "But Owen talked to me. He reminded me that not many people get the chance to play college football. He said, 'You're on scholarship. You won't regret it.' And I didn't. I loved every second of it. I wish I could go back and play football again."

Although Owen had found a new brotherhood among the Quakers, it somehow fell short of the relationships that high school football had provided. Reluctant to abandon that identity, he continued to follow his high school team closely. In his room at Penn, reading a story online in his hometown newspaper, *The Morning Call*, about the traditional Parkland-Whitehall rivalry and the upcoming game between the two schools, he became incensed that Whitehall coach Tony Trisciani had boasted, "Yes, we can beat Parkland." Owen was inspired to deliver one more pep talk to the Trojans, just as he had done as team captain. He wrote an email addressed to Parkland head coach Jim Morgans. Offensive line coach Paul Hagadus was cc'd on the missive, which had the subject line: "The Whitehall Game." It was sent at 4:12 a.m. on Wednesday, October 31, 2007. Friends later said they could imagine him pacing in his room at Penn before sitting down at his computer to write a locker room speech that would be shared with Parkland players by coaches for several years before each Whitehall game.

This fucking pissed me off so badly when I read this. It made me sick. This quote just illustrates how big of a rivalry and how important of a game Whitehall is. You need to understand that this is more than just a game, it's personal. This game doesn't reflect records, or past seasons, or hype. It reflects business. It doesn't matter if they're 7–2 or 2–7, this game is a glorified way to just personally kick the fucking shit out of a bunch of punch-bitch wannabees who think they can beat you. It will be four quarters of tough, hard-nosed football and this is how it should be because Parkland = Power. WE don't do fancy plays or finesse the ball down the field. We grind it out, pound it out with strength, technique and determination. We win the battles in the trenches, where the game is won and lost. We run hard, play hard, and succeed. We don't change our game plan. We fight, we battle, we persevere, and we win. This is Parkland Football. Last time I checked, these bastards haven't won this game in a while; and you know what? It's your job to make them remember why. When you get ready for this game in practice, or in the weight room, on Thursday practice, even in school Friday, remember: You Guys Represent Us! YOU REPRESENT PARKLAND FOOTBALL! I know I'm old hat and I've moved on, but trust me, like any coach can tell you, there is nothing like high school football, and there sure as hell isn't anything like Parkland Football. I am so proud to be a product of Parkland Football because Parkland Football represents what true high school football is.

I want you guys to read this and think about what this game means to you. Think of how you will feel after you dominate their souls and pound them into the ground. Think of how you need to execute and work hard in order to send a message. Think of the focus and preparation you need in order to win. Think of how you want to look back on this game in the years to come. Then just play Parkland Football.

CHAPTER 9

PLAYING THROUGH
THE PAIN

IT IS A TERM SOLIDLY ENTRENCHED in the University of Pennsylvania campus culture, a part of the lexicon simultaneously embraced and criticized. Penn Face refers to the masking behavior—the public face—that students at Penn present to the world to maintain a perfect image while hiding feelings of inadequacy, failure, or vulnerability.[1]

By spring 2009, at the end of his sophomore year, Owen Thomas had his Penn Face firmly in place.

The idea of the Penn Face came under scrutiny after the increasing number of student suicides at Penn peaked with seven student deaths in the course of the 2013–2014 and 2014–2015 academic years. It led to a campuswide questioning of the culture of perfection that pervaded the Penn campus. Following those suicides, the university administration responded with a mental health task force to examine the campus culture and make recommendations for improvements to mental health services. Grassroots student organizations were founded to deal with mental health issues and with what could be a demoralizingly competitive campus culture.[2]

The response was five years too late for Owen. As an athlete, he already had a warrior's mentality that precluded letting down teammates, friends, and family. It was part of a personal commitment to never display anything but his best. It's a long-acknowledged trait among competitive athletes that they are willing to "play through pain." With that mind-set, the concept of showing his Penn Face to the world while hiding personal challenges made sense to Owen. Indeed, after years embracing the idea of being an academic and athletic warrior, it almost seemed natural. And underneath it all, unknown to anyone, there was a brain already riddled with macerated tissue, more than twenty lesions indicative of CTE. Like a bad knee predisposes a player to injury, the presence of CTE in Owen's brain could predispose him to depression and memory problems. Damage in his prefrontal cortex could contribute to difficulties with impulsivity.[3] This physical liability combined with the student culture at Penn began to erode Owen's usually positive nature as he transitioned from his sophomore to his junior year.

|||||||||||||

Abbie and Owen had continued the romantic relationship that had started when they were high school seniors. They maintained their romance through the first two years of college, text messaging four times a day, visiting each other many weekends and during holiday breaks. Abbie was the person to whom he first confided his struggles to compete academically at Penn. Recalling his status as an intellectual superstar in high school, he had told her, "I'm not Owen Thomas anymore. I'm at Penn—where everyone is Owen Thomas."

In truth, failure sometimes meant a B or a C instead of the A grades that previously had been the norm. By spring 2009, seriously feeling the stress of balancing athletics and academics, he began struggling with depression and started seeing a counselor—something he confessed to her with some embarrassment. "I said, 'I support that. I can't help you as much as a counselor could,'" Abbie recalled.

He continued the counseling appointments in summer 2009, remaining in Philadelphia to take summer classes, work a job in the campus gym, and maintain his strength and conditioning regimen. Dave Macknet, who had just moved into the house, lived with him. "We were the only ones living in the house that summer. He was taking classes, I was doing research at the hospital," Dave said. Whatever personal problems Owen might have felt, Dave saw no evidence of them. Owen appeared as he had always been to his teammates. "We would meet in the weight room at night," Macknet said. "I loved working out with him because of the intensity he brought and the effort he brought."

The start of fall semester saw the return of the other roommates to Baltimore Avenue. With Macknet added to the crew, it promised to be another year of balancing academics with unbridled fun.

The fall 2009 football season would be a golden one, with the Quakers' only defeats being two losses in September in nonconference games against Villanova University and Lafayette College. Owen and high school friend Marc Quilling, now playing for Lafayette's Leopards, would trade barbs about the loss. The Quakers would go undefeated for the rest of the season to win the Ivy League title, clinching it with a 34–0 win over Cornell at home at Franklin Field. Owen would earn second team All-Ivy status recording twenty-nine tackles and finishing second in the league with six sacks.

In team photos recording the celebration that followed clinching the Ivy League title, there's no sign of depression on Owen's face. He beams, grinning at the camera, his flaming hair—now cropped short—bright among his dark-haired teammates. It would be a high point of the semester, a positive memory that his teammates would burnish.

Owen's relationship with Abbie ended shortly after his birthday in September. High school friend Mike Fay, traveling on a darkened team bus across Ohio as the Kent State team returned from an away game, received a phone call from Owen. Mike still dated Jess, Abbie's twin sister, and the four had been inseparable. "It was the last time I talked with him," Mike said. "He said, 'Fay, I just don't want to lose you as a friend. I'm not with Abbie anymore. I just don't want to lose you as friend.' And I told him, 'Of course not.'"

Abbie quietly characterizes the end of the relationship as a natural outcome of going to different colleges and leading different lives. "We grew apart," she says. A few of Owen's male friends chalked it up to him needing more freedom.

Academically, he seemed on an even keel. With Abbie gone, there was no one in whom he could confidently confide his academic problems. In some classes, at least, Owen was succeeding. The fall 2009 semester was the time when he became the memorable student in Adam Grant's Organizational Behavior class.

For the first time, Owen was a single college guy, free to party and to join his friends prowling the bars on the streets surrounding Penn's campus in University City. He and his teammates were regulars at Smokey Joe's—called Smokes in Penn parlance. If they weren't there, they might be at Sansom's or the Blarney Stone.

Owen coined a term for the unattached young women he would meet: lady birds. Visiting Marc Quilling at Lafayette College, they made the rounds, stopping at parties in various student houses off campus. Owen wanted to stop at any house where he heard noises indicating celebration. If Marc demurred, saying he didn't know the inhabitants, Owen ignored him, striding confidently up to the door and knocking.

"Who are you?" questioned the party's host as he opened the door to find Owen, an imposing figure with his red hair, and Marc, still standing down on the sidewalk.

"We're here to party," Owen would announce, inviting himself in. It often worked.

On another visit, when the guys were hitting the bars in the College Hill neighborhood surrounding Lafayette, Owen took Marc aside after dancing with a girl. "He said, 'I think this lady bird over here is digging me,'" Marc said, grinning at the memory.

In no time, Owen became the chief party animal at Baltimore Avenue. Another raucous New Year's Eve bash ushered in 2010. "In January, he was almost on top of the world, going out all the time, seeing girls," recalled Dave Macknet. Although always one for a good time, Owen's partying had reached a new level, one that sometimes bordered on recklessness. In hindsight, the tendency of depressed individuals to self-medicate with alcohol or drugs seems likely. But at the time, he appeared to be a typical college student having too good of a time.

Penn State, which Owen's close friend Kristen Dota attended, was a favorite stop in the 2009–2010 year. One trip was to the annual celebration dubbed State Patty's Day. Started in 2007 as an alternative way for Penn State students to celebrate St. Patrick's Day when the holiday fell during spring break, the event had become an annual day of drunken revelry in the streets of State College, Pennsylvania. In 2010, it was observed on Saturday, February 27, and would result in 160 arrests.

Owen and his roommates set out early from Philadelphia to join the fun in the place dubbed Happy Valley. It was a snowy day and Justin Cosgrove—not the best driver—was behind the wheel with Owen, Luke DeLuca, and Adam Triglia on board. En route, the car did a 360-degree turn on an icy road and ended up in a ditch. The inhabitants of the car were terrified. Owen was the first to speak: "All right, let's get out of here." With some careful maneuvering in the four-wheel drive vehicle, they were soon on their way.

Once in State College, the four-man contingent from Penn would join several of Owen's high school friends who were in town for the party. Marc Quilling had come from Lafayette. Even Jamie Pagliaro made the trip from William & Mary, more than three hundred miles away in Virginia. Drinking started on arrival and continued throughout the day. With the help of cell phones, it was easy to track down a buddy amid the hordes that had descended on the town.

Jamie answered his phone to hear Owen's voice: "Where are you?"

Jamie gave him the name of the street where he had paused to take the call and Owen responded, "No you're not, because that's where I am."

"And I turned around and there was Owen standing there talking to me," Jamie said.

The most unforgettable event happened late in the day. Recorded in a video on Marc Quilling's cell phone, Owen is in the emergency room, his gaze slightly unfocused. A nurse, barely visible on camera, is urging him to say the alphabet backward. Marc's voice, off camera, urges him on. "Come on, Owen." The nurse reaches out to bat Marc's hand away when she realizes that he's taking a video of his friend. Unfazed, he continues recording.

A very drunk Owen had landed in the emergency room— one of 103 State Patty's Day revelers who would end up there that day—after falling and hitting his head on the edge of a table. Upon Owen's arrival at Mount Nittany Medical Center, the nurse who admitted him asked if he'd been drinking. Owen, polite even when inebriated, responded, "Yes, ma'am. All day." The response became a favorite among his friends, repeated over and over again.

Still photos took up where the video ended, a chronicle of Owen's treatment also saved on Marc's phone. One shows Owen with gauze wrapped around his head. A second is a close-up of the gash on the crown of his head, mended with surgical staples, seen between the spikes of his short red hair. The third is a shot of Owen posing with a guy who has blood visible around his right ear, holding up a bag filled with ice. The guy had lost part of his ear in a bar fight—a feat worthy of a photo, Owen insisted.

At some point, the photos ended up on Facebook, reflecting the kind of drunken behavior typical of twenty-something guys. But some of Owen's female friends asked Marc to take it down—among them Emily Toth DeLuca and the Benner twins. "That's not Owen," they would say.

In the weeks that followed that late February weekend, more than one woman who knew Owen well would take up the refrain. "That's not Owen." Women who knew him sensed that something was not quite right with their friend in the first months of 2010. One was Jamie Berkowitz, Owen's first high school girlfriend, who had dated him before his relationship with Abbie. Jamie had gone to college at West Chester University, not far from Philadelphia. It was another stop on the party trail for Owen that spring, and Jamie remembered the visit, the details becoming more significant to her in hindsight.

Watching Owen at the party, something seemed amiss. Concerned, she pulled aside Marc Quilling, who had accompanied him.

"There's something wrong with Owen," Jamie said.

"Nah, he's just Owen being Owen," Marc said, shrugging off her concern to rejoin the fun.

His answer did nothing to alleviate her concern.

"I thought that I was crazy for thinking what I was thinking," Jamie recalled. "But when I looked in his eyes, I saw a complete blankness when he was waiting to speak. It was almost like you could see his brain trying to process everything around him."

Jamie also noted that he was more aggressively hitting on women in social settings. "And it wasn't in his cute, sincere Owen way. It was almost a prerogative. Like he was obligated. It got to the point where he'd overstep and get annoying." Before the weekend was over, Owen came pounding on her door, demanding a place to sleep, and displaying an aggression that seemed unlike the boy she'd known. She couldn't get the phrase out of her head: Owen's not Owen. Something's wrong with Owen. The women were seeing a pattern similar to what the wives of former NFL players who were later found to have CTE would report over the years: impulsive, out-of-character actions on the part of someone they thought they knew.

As winter ended and spring made its slow, green entrance, the weeks creeping toward April, Owen's teammates started to note the anxiety in their friend. The Penn Face was slipping. Wharton students were lining up prestigious internships for the summer between their junior and senior years. Owen was having no luck. He paid a visit to Adam Grant, the popular professor who'd noted Owen's exceptional ability just six months before. Grant asked Owen questions about the kinds of organizations he was interested in interning with, told him he'd be happy to make some introductions, and asked him to send him the latest copy of his resume. "You know, he never followed up, and so I just kind of assumed that he had found something," Grant said.

It was on the heels of the 2008 recession, and millennials like Owen were keenly aware that the job opportunities and financial security that were a given to previous generations could well elude them.

Owen's mother commiserated with her son. She was between ministerial jobs, so she knew what it was like to be coming up short when looking for a position. And she offered him advice. "I talked to him on the phone once, I think it was in February," Kathy said. "And he said he was really struggling, and I said, 'Owen, you have to realize, you have such high standards, you give 150 percent. You don't have to give 150 percent. There are people who get by, who give 80 percent. Can you try and get that into perspective?'"

With the start of spring football, Jake Peterson found Owen had changed. "I remember looking back at our conversations. They started to get tough. He was kind of frustrated. And feeling overwhelmed with things. He wasn't playing like he usually did. He started making a lot of mistakes," Peterson said. "One of the hard things for me was seeing it was happening."

Owen's conversations had a consistent theme: he was falling short. One day Daniel Lipschutz found himself having lunch alone with Owen. It was rare, Daniel said, because the upperclassmen on the football team usually traveled in packs.

"I remembered him being very stressed out about school. In Wharton, it was a very intense on-campus recruitment period. The students would all wear suits and would be networking. For a lot of guys on the football team that was especially stressful; they already had a packed schedule," Daniel said. "Our whole conversation was a combination of how that was going and how he was doing in his classes. For someone who was usually vibrant, he seemed worn down by school. He was not feeling very good about himself. I was surprised he lacked confidence."

In early April, some of Owen's high school friends stopped to visit him on their way home to the Lehigh Valley for the Easter holiday weekend. The next day, on their way out of Philadelphia, they noted that something seemed wrong. Owen was not himself. Thinking back on the visit left them feeling uneasy. One of them brushed it off, thinking the change might be due to the imminent start of finals. Another noted that they had arrived late the night before. Maybe Owen was tired.

What those friends had been sensing was becoming clear to his roommates. "He was in a dark place. He really withdrew from everybody. He wouldn't do activities he normally would do with us. He was talking more about his concern about grades and how he was failing classes. . . . He wasn't sleeping as much," said Dave Macknet. He and some of the others went to the football coaching staff and expressed their concerns.

As the end of the semester neared, his roommates also noticed something that they, too, would be haunted by later. Owen entered the room with some very pronounced marks on his neck that looked like rug burns. When they questioned him, Dave recalled, "He told us he cut himself shaving."

|||||||||||||

April 26, a gray and rainy day, matched the mood of students at the University of Pennsylvania. Temperatures hovered in the fifties, chilly with no hint of spring to lighten their mood as they prepared for exams the following week. The next day would be the last day of classes for the spring 2010 term. The young men living on Baltimore Avenue spent most of their free time in the library, avoiding the distractions of partying or playing video games together.

Looking back, Owen's friends wondered if he had chosen a time when the house would be empty. No one remembered seeing him at lunch. But when they found him, it looked as if he had been impulsive. His computer was on. His wallet was on the desk. There was no note. His phone was still in his pocket when he attached a football belt to the top molding of his closet door, put it around his neck and hung himself.

The medical examiner's report states that the call for an ambulance went out at 1:59 p.m.,[4] shortly after Justin Cosgrove had returned to the house. On the second floor at the end of the hall, just a few steps away from his room, he noticed Owen's door was open a crack and went to say hello. Inside he saw Owen hanging. A surge of adrenaline kicked him into action. He used a pair of scissors on the desk to cut Owen down, placed a frenzied call to 911 and began performing CPR. Owen wasn't responding.

When the ambulance arrived at the trauma bay at the Hospital of the University of Pennsylvania at 2:28 p.m., Owen's pupils were fixed and dilated and he was without a pulse. Adrenaline administered en route had no effect. Hospital staff continued to attempt to resuscitate him for ten more minutes, administering more drugs and continuing chest compressions. He was pronounced dead at 2:38 p.m.[5]

By that point, many were waiting for news. Friends would always remember where they were when they learned he had taken his life.

||||||||||||

Luke DeLuca was at Van Pelt Library, where he had retreated from his roommates so he could get work done. He saw the call from Adam Triglia pop up on his phone and briefly considered ignoring it; he had a test the next day.

"You've got to come home," Adam said.

"No way, man, I've got a lot of stuff to do," Luke answered, puzzled by the urgency in his roommate's voice.

"Owen tried to kill himself," Adam said. Luke scrambled to pack up his books and notes and sprinted nearly a mile to their house. He expected to find his other roommates talking to Owen, calming him after averting a tragedy. But by the time he arrived, so had the police and the ambulance. Quickly, Coach Jim Schaefer, Owen's line coach, and others from the Penn coaching staff, somehow alerted, had run from the stadium to the house. After the ambulance sped away, Owen's friends went to the police station to make statements, and await word.

Abbie Benner and her twin, Jess, who shared an off-campus apartment, also were heading into finals at Millersville University, more than an hour from Penn. Abbie felt nauseous. "I went to class and I called Jess and I said, 'I feel like my throat is really tight. I feel like I have to throw up, but I can't,'" Abbie said. She went back to her apartment.

Jess got a call from Mike Fay. He shared the news; Owen had attempted suicide. That was how all of the friends he had loved, now living in so many places, would first hear. That he had tried to kill himself. Fate, it appeared, was giving them a few hours to get used to the idea before they would have to process the unthinkable.

"We didn't even know he was dead," Jess said.

In the age of cell phones, so many friends were connected in so many places. The news spread quickly. A Parkland High graduate who was dating a Penn football player called friends in their close-knit circle.

Marc Quilling was among those she contacted. "I was hysterical," Marc said, using a word not many young men in their twenties would easily use to describe their emotions. "One of my roommates knocked on my door to see if I was OK." He called his mother to come and take him home. But first he got in touch with some of the former Trojans.

Jamie Pagliaro at William & Mary in Williamsburg, Virginia, also received a call. A deeply shaken Jamie immediately prepared to drive home to Pennsylvania.

"I was about to get in my car. My buddy took my keys and said, 'You're not going,'" Pags said. He called the Tribe's offensive line coach, Bob Solderitch, a fellow Pennsylvanian who'd attended Parkland's rival, Whitehall High. "He rushed over to my house. His friend had done the same thing—killed himself. So he sat me down and talked to me. That was actually what helped me the most: my 'O' coach talking to me."

Solderitch insisted, "You can't drive. It's a six-hour drive." Jamie's roommates stepped in. Despite the fact that finals were beginning, they drove him to Washington, DC, where his father and grandfather met them to take Jamie the rest of the way back to Schnecksville.

Members of the Penn football team were summoned to a special team meeting. Gathered in a dim room in the Towne Building across from Franklin Field, the players learned that the man they had unanimously elected team captain just a week before was dead. After the announcement, they sat together, the sound of young men weeping filling the room.

The principal called Ryan Hulmes to the office at Parkland High School. He had some bad news about Owen Thomas. Hulmes would be the one to tell head coach Jim Morgans.

Before the day was over, Marc Quilling showed up in the high school weight room, Hulmes said. "Quilling knew. You could see it in his eyes," Hulmes recalled. "He just wanted to be up here with us." The relationships in the weight room had been built on the love of a game and a brotherhood that surpassed the win-loss record. Now it was being reinforced by a shared loss that no one could fathom.

The next day, they told the Parkland football team. Most of the upperclassmen had been freshmen when Owen was a senior. He was their larger-than-life hero, a big brother and the player they had admired and tried to emulate.

"I broke it to the team," Hulmes said. "It wasn't the days of texting and Twitter and all that jazz yet. Some knew, most didn't. I'd say 90 percent didn't. Michael Zaccaro, God bless the kid, he was the spiritual leader. He asked if he could lead us in prayer. And he did. We stayed down there for two periods, kind of leaning on each other. The kids were more there for us than we were there for them. I had a lot of kids after that, checking on me, emailing me, saying, 'I know you're going through a rough time.'"

That day, more of Owen's former Parkland teammates—his oldest friends—would join Marc Quilling in visiting their former coaches. "I think one of the most heartbreaking things was when I saw Coach Hulmes's face," said Jamie. "I remember when we all got together that day, before we went over to the Thomases' house to see Mrs. Thomas and Mr. Thomas and Morgan. We all went over to the weight room to see Coach Morgans and all them. I don't think I've ever seen Coach Hulmes show any emotion except angry or happy. And he just broke down when he came and saw us."

||||||||||||

Tom Thomas was in his office at Union United Church of Christ. His window looked out on part of the cemetery where generations of congregants are buried. Mondays were normally slow days, coming after a Sunday when he led two services. Tom doesn't remember how he first heard Owen was in the hospital, but he received the news before he got an official call from Penn.

"Mike Fay must have talked to somebody. Or somebody saw Mike Fay's Facebook or something. I learned Owen was in the hospital. I don't remember exactly how I got it." Tom speaks quietly, in measured tones. His training in pastoral counseling, his experience walking so many others through such moments, helps him to keep his emotions in check. "My first reaction was to call his position coach, Coach Schaefer. I had the coach's cell phone, so I called, and I didn't hear anything."

Tom first thought that Owen—as much of a daredevil on his bicycle as he was on the football field—might have had an accident riding on the Philadelphia streets. Then the university chaplain called with news that his youngest son had hung himself.

He quickly drove home and burst into the house, shouting the news to his son Matt, who was home. Tom initially could not reach Kathy, who was in a meeting. Morgan was finishing his semester at East Stroudsburg University. He called Morgan's girlfriend, Brittany, the girl his son would later marry. Tom asked her to break the news to Morgan and stay with him.

Tom and Kathy headed to Penn as soon as she arrived at home. Pulling in at the University of Pennsylvania hospital, they were met by the head of security, coincidentally, a man Owen had recently interviewed for a class project. He arranged for them to park by the ambulances outside the emergency room, avoiding the rigmarole of parking at the massive hospital. "Two chaplains came and talked to us and then the doctor came and talked to us," Tom recalls. He pauses before delivering a pathetic understatement. "It was a horrible day, a horrible, horrible day." He does not mention what the medical examiner's report confirms: that he was the person who identified his son's body.

Later, Tom recalled the phone call he had received from Owen the day before, in which he talked about being overwhelmed by his approaching exams. "It was a weary voice. A weepy, teary kind of voice. I was exhausted because we had just finished the (United Church of Christ) Penn Northeast Conference two-day gathering and I'd done worship and I was so exhausted on Sunday night and I thought, 'Should I go down or should I not?'"

There would be an autopsy. It would be a few days before Owen's body would be brought home for burial. Tom and Kathy headed back to the Lehigh Valley. In the years that followed, the exact sequence of events on one of the worst days of their life would blur a bit. Kathy no longer remembers whether she received the call in the car en route to Allentown or back home on Jonagold Road. But she remembers what the caller—a young man named Chris Nowinski—would ask her within hours of learning her youngest child had killed himself. "Mrs. Thomas," he would say. "Can we have Owen's brain?"

CHAPTER 10

TESTIMONY

AT A MUSCULAR SIX FEET, FIVE INCHES TALL, Chris Nowinski is an intimidating presence who towers over most people. It's the kind of presence that comes in handy on a football field or in the ring as a pro wrestler—both athletic careers that he had pursued in his early twenties. A football player in his high school near Chicago, he went on to play for the Harvard Crimson before graduating from the Ivy League school with a degree in sociology. Although he initially followed a traditional path after graduation by working for a life sciences consulting firm, he decided to explore his interest in professional wrestling, a world that married his athletic talents with an earlier interest in theater. Adopting the wrestling persona of Chris Harvard, Nowinski put his imposing physical presence, coupled with a larger-than-life personality that flaunted his Ivy League superiority with a stream of verbal boasts about his intellect, to work on World Wrestling Entertainment's *Monday Night Raw*. Then an opponent kicked him in the head. He ended up with post-concussion syndrome, a debilitating condition characterized by chronic headaches, difficulty sleeping, and memory problems. It ended his wrestling career.[1]

The concussion would lead Nowinski to his life's work as an activist raising awareness about the dangers of concussions among athletes—particularly young athletes. He wrote a book about the problem, *Head Games: Football's Concussion Crisis from the NFL to Youth Leagues*. With Robert Cantu, the neurologist who had treated his post-concussion syndrome, Nowinski founded the Concussion Legacy Foundation and the Boston University CTE Center. Early on in the evolving field of CTE research, he took on a role that most would find difficult, or at the very least discomfiting. Nowinski described his role in a 2017 TED talk, in which he introduced himself saying, "Odds are, if you've met me in the last five years, I've asked you after a few minutes, a bit of an odd question: Can I have your brain?"[2]

The first time he'd posed the question, it was in a phone call to the eighty-eight-year-old mother of Philadelphia Eagles safety Andre Waters. Waters had shot himself in the head in November 2006 after months of exhibiting signs of depression. Nowinski had sought the brain on a hunch that Waters—who said he stopped counting his concussions at fifteen—had CTE. It turned out Nowinski was right, and soon he was spending his days scanning newspapers and the internet for obituaries of former players and asking bereaved families to donate their loved ones' brains for research.

By the time Owen Thomas died in 2010, Nowinski had made a lot more calls asking for brains. Although he had never met Owen Thomas, there had been something familiar about his case, something that Nowinski identified with when he learned of his suicide.

Interviewed in the documentary film based on his book, Nowinski remembers hearing about Owen's death. "For me it was a special case. This was an Ivy League defensive lineman. I was an Ivy League defensive lineman. It was like losing one of our own."

Owen Thomas officially became part of the football concussion controversy less than six months after he died—and seventeen days before what would have been his twenty-second birthday. Chris Nowinski's hunch had paid off when he learned of Owen's death and contacted the Thomas family to ask that his brain be donated to Boston University's CTE research. His would become a landmark case in the unfolding crisis.

"At that point, most cases had been found in professional football players, and it opened up the idea in a lot of people's heads that this is affecting just good, nice kids who are playing football for the right reasons, who are also smart and successful," says Nowinski, who had become CEO of the Concussion Legacy Foundation that he had cofounded.

The headline in the September 13, 2010, *New York Times* stated: "Suicide Reveals Signs of a Disease Seen in N.F.L." The story, written by Alan Schwarz, a writer who had followed the CTE story from its beginnings, recounted that an autopsy of Owen's brain revealed that he had chronic traumatic encephalopathy, the brain disease until then linked primarily to professional players. The story outlined the significance of the discovery in two key paragraphs:

Thomas is the youngest and first amateur football player to be found with clear C.T.E., which is linked with cognitive impairment, depression and ultimately dementia. One 18-year-old former high school player who died two years ago, and whose name has been withheld by the Boston University researchers at his family's request, had only incipient traces of the disease.

Later in the story, perhaps an even more disturbing detail was noted:

Thomas never had a diagnosis of a concussion on or off the football field or even complained of a headache, his parents said, although they acknowledged he was the kind of player who might have ignored the symptoms to stay on the field. Because of this, several doctors said, his CTE—whose only known cause is repetitive brain trauma—must have developed from concussions he dismissed or from the thousands of subconcussive collisions he withstood in his dozen years of football, most of them while his brain was developing.

After the *Times* broke the news about Owen, subsequent stories appeared on ESPN and in *Sports Illustrated*; *The Los Angeles Times*; Owen's hometown newspaper, *The Morning Call*; and *The Philadelphia Inquirer*. The news also was covered on National Public Radio and dozens of other newspaper and television newscasts. *The Daily Pennsylvanian*, the University of Pennsylvania student newspaper, carried a story quoting the *Times* article, Owen's mother, and experts at the University of California, Los Angeles's Brain Injury Research Center.

At the time of Owen's death, CTE researchers were reluctant to say definitively that the CTE diagnosis meant that the disease was a prevailing factor causing Owen's depression and subsequent suicide. At that time, Boston University researcher Ann McKee had found the disease in nineteen out of twenty brains of former NFL players—and most of them had far more advanced cases. Still, there was a mounting body of evidence that CTE manifested itself with depression and problems with impulse control—both seen in Owen's behavior leading up to his death and evident in the very manner in which he took his life. In the years since his death, researchers have begun to establish a direct link between suicide and brain trauma. "Not every case of mental instability is related to physical injury to the brain, but I think we're seeing more and more that repeated trauma increases the risk for suicide," Ann McKee said. "There's military literature now that shows higher lifetime exposure to trauma increases the risk of suicide. So I'm thinking they're more and more connected. But we need to do a lot more study to make that determination."

One other striking factor about the discovery of the disease in Owen's brain stunned McKee and other researchers. The brains in which the disease had been identified by the Boston physicians up until that time had come from former players who had shown signs of severe impairment before their deaths. That impairment had led their families to donate their brains. In Owen's case, although there was evidence of depression and some impetuous or impulsive behavior for a short time before his suicide, he clearly had been living the active, normal life of a twenty-one-year-old. And yet the disease in his brain was already quite pronounced. McKee recalled, "I found between twenty and thirty of these lesions and most of them were in the frontal lobe. So the difference between stage one and stage two is mostly that these lesions are much more frequent. And in Owen's brain, as I recall, in practically every section we had some abnormality."

In July 2010, a poster appeared in NFL team locker rooms, mandated by the league. It's message, targeting players, was clear: "Concussions and conditions resulting from repeated brain injury can change your life and your family's life forever." In September of that year, the NFL gave $30 million to the National Institutes of Health for research into brain trauma.[3]

The mounting number of cases of CTE among former NFL players would keep the issue alive. And as the evidence about the dangers of the disease among football players and other athletes grew, the significance of Owen's case also increased.

|||||||||||||

The battered Parkland football helmet sat on the polished wood table in the US House of Representatives. The helmet was nicked by many collisions sustained in games and festooned with the stars awarded to Owen for valor on the field during his high school football career, including those earned from Coach Morgans as player of the week. Kathy Brearley sat near the helmet that represented one-third of the twelve years her son had played the game.

It was September 22, 2010, just a week after the results of the examination were announced revealing that Owen had

CTE. Kathy was testifying before the House Committee on Education and Labor in the third hearing on federal legislation that aimed to reduce and more safely manage concussions in student athletes. She had agreed to testify at the request of Chris Nowinski, Ann McKee, and other staff at the Sports Legacy Foundation.

"If my son Owen was sitting with us today, he would say, 'Mom, it's OK. Don't make a fuss.' He would cringe at the thought of being the center of so much attention," Kathy said in her crisp English accent. "Although an excellent wordsmith, Owen would adhere to the unspoken football rule that words are used sparingly. Actions speak for themselves. In that ancient motif of oratory—Athens versus warrior Sparta—today Owen would stand with Sparta."[4]

Noting that she only learned about football after coming to the United States in 1982, she shared the details of her son's death by suicide at the University of Pennsylvania. In less than a hundred words, her voice steady, she described how he had hung himself, then moved on with her testimony. "My first purpose," Kathy continued, "is to put a human face on the disease called chronic traumatic encephalopathy."

Owen's untimely death generates a new set of questions to be addressed by future CTE research. He had no known concussions at any time when playing soccer, basketball, baseball, or football. To our knowledge Owen never used steroids or abused drugs or alcohol. He had never been involved in a car accident and had never been hospitalized. He had no history of depression. We have no family history of depression or dementia. Owen never complained of headaches or acted strangely.

The only possible explanation we can see for the presence of CTE is that Owen started to play football at the age of nine. He was a very physical and intense player who threw himself into every sport he played. In precollege football he often played offense and defense and was on the field for much of the game. Maybe he had mild concussions that he never reported—that would be Owen, anxious to return to the game, not a coach pressurizing him. No one could ever pressurize Owen to do anything. Or maybe CTE is the cumulative effect of multiple subconcussions, compounded by some as yet unknown genetic component.[5]

Her next words reflected thoughts that Kathy returned to often after Owen's death: because of CTE, her son's future—if he had lived—would have been radically different than what he and his parents had imagined. Owen would have lived the greatly diminished life faced by hundreds of retired NFL players, grappling with memory loss, depression, and anger, and yet he would never have played a minute of pro football.

"Whatever the explanation, the fact is that we now know Owen—the recipient of his high school's Eisenhower Award for leadership—faced an increasingly circumscribed future as his brain disease progressed. We would surely have loved and supported him no matter what the cost, but the bright future to which he aspired would have eluded him," his mother stated.[6]

Noting that "football is indeed the spirit of Sparta acted out in our own time, a careful crafting of male athletic skill and teamwork," Kathy went on to tell members of the committee that legislation was needed that would require high schools to protect their athletes while preserving the game. "In speaking out about Owen's brain disease, it is my hope that parents and coaches will unite to improve the safety of younger players, so football can continue to be a powerful and exciting sport that unites families and communities all across the United States," she said.[7]

Pennsylvania congressman Todd Russell Platts praised Kathy for her testimony, telling her, "You'll make sure we do better for all the Owens out there."

Owen's name would again be entered into the *Congressional Record* a little more than a year later. On October 19, 2011, the

Senate Committee on Commerce, Science, and Transportation held a hearing on concussions and the marketing of sports equipment. It was an important and timely topic, as coaches, parents, and athletes pondered how helmets and other equipment might ameliorate the effects of jarring hits to the head in many sports, most importantly soccer and football. This time it would be Ann McKee, the CTE researcher who had discovered the condition in Owen's brain postmortem, who would tell his story, using it as a cautionary tale, responding to those who might think that only professional athletes should be concerned about CTE.

McKee first gave the senators a short course in concussions, traumatic brain injury, and CTE. After outlining her expertise in the field of CTE research (including diagnosing fifty-eight deceased athletes with CTE), she noted two specific cases that she felt dramatically illustrated concerns about CTE. The first was former Chicago Bears defensive back Dave Duerson, who began playing football at age eight and suffered eleven concussions in his NFL career. After retiring from football, he enjoyed a successful career—for a time. McKee continued, "At the age of forty-six, he experienced financial difficulties and the dissolution of his marriage. He became hot-tempered, physically and verbally abusive. He developed memory lapses, mood swings, and piercing headaches. And on February 17, 2011, he killed himself inside his Florida apartment. He left instructions to donate his brain to my laboratory, and my examination showed that he was suffering from moderately severe CTE, even though he was only fifty years old."[8]

McKee then cited another case, one that was significant for a different reason. "Another example is Owen Thomas, a defensive end for the University of Pennsylvania who played football since age nine. One day in the spring of 2010, he called his parents and told them he was stressed by school and having trouble with several of his courses. And two days later, he hanged himself in his off-campus apartment.

"When I looked at Owen's brain, I saw unmistakable changes of early CTE. In fact, if you compare the brain of Owen Thomas to the brain of Dave Duerson, there was remarkably similar, although milder, pathology, suggesting that if Owen Thomas had lived another thirty years his CTE would have progressed to the advanced stage demonstrated by Dave Duerson."

McKee would go on to cite subsequent findings, including early-stage CTE found in a seventeen-year-old high school football player who died after returning to play three weeks after incurring a concussion. In concluding her testimony, she stated, "However, there are many things that we do not understand about CTE. We do not understand or we do not know the exact incidence and prevalence of this disorder, even though we now clearly understand that this disease exists, and it is surprisingly common.

"What factors determine who will develop CTE?" she continued.

> How many concussions, how many subconcussive injuries, how close together the injuries, how severe, and at what age? All of these are aspects of the disease that are unknown at this time. Importantly, we do not know how to diagnose this disease in living individuals, how to stop its progression, or how to reverse its course. But we can make important changes to prevent this disease from developing in young athletes, and those changes include understanding what a concussion is, recognition of concussion when it occurs, and proper medical management of concussion after it happens.[9]

Dramatic testimony like McKee's, delivered in front of Congress, seemed to make little impact on football fans. But the actions of beloved former players kept the head injury issue alive for the public. Late in 2011, former Atlanta Falcons safety Ray Easterling would file suit against the NFL for its deception regarding the seriousness of brain injury. Eventually the suit would be joined by more than 4,500 players. In April 2012, Easterling committed suicide and was subsequently found to have CTE.[10] The next month, in May 2012, former San Diego Chargers linebacker Junior Seau shot himself at age forty-three, two years after retiring. Like Dave Duerson, he, too, had exhibited increasingly erratic behavior. Like Duerson, he was found to have CTE.

After Seau's death, Owen's mother, Kathy, would write on the "RIP Owen Thomas" Facebook page, addressing her son, who had also been a linebacker: "I guess you and Junior Seau have something to talk about. I'm so sorry we failed to protect you both. We're trying to do better for new kids coming along."

| | | | | | | | | | | | |

Her testimony—and Ann McKee's—had advanced the debate about concussions and safety measures for young athletes among lawmakers. But federal legislation addressing the issue—introduced in April 2015 as the Protecting Student Athletes from Concussions Act—would be first referred to the House Committee for Education and the Workforce and then to the subcommittee on Early Childhood, Elementary and Secondary Education where it would languish. A similar bill would be reintroduced in July 2017. Both the 2015 and 2017 versions would require states to enact measures compelling public schools to develop plans for concussion safety and management. Initiatives to improve education about preventing and diagnosing concussions would come from laws and initiatives on the state level and from rule changes and educational efforts advanced by organizations as diverse as the Centers for Disease Control, the NCAA, and youth football programs. The NFL made a show of announcing its own program to prevent head injuries in youth football. In August 2012, the league announced the Heads Up Football program, offered in conjunction with USA Football, an online coaching education site. An NFL statement announcing the program said it "emphasizes a smarter and safer way to play and teach youth football, including proper tackling and taking the head out of the game." Perhaps the closest thing to an effective law related to concussions is the Zackery Lystedt Law, named for a thirteen-year-old football player in the Tahoma School District in Washington State who nearly died after being allowed to return to play too soon after sustaining a concussion. By 2017, all fifty states and Washington, DC, had enacted versions of the law, which requires coaches and other staff to have yearly training to recognize concussions, and requires athletes to leave games if they are suspected of having a concussion. The law also stipulates that a licensed healthcare professional must clear a player to return to play.[11]

Research published in 2017 in the *American Journal of Public Health* showed the rate of recurrent concussions had decreased. But the same research study also showed that there has been no decrease in new concussions among young athletes. The finding would come as no surprise to many who love football. The helmet that gave silent testimony while Kathy Brearley spoke to Congress in 2010 reflected the reality for many young players: they were willing to risk injury for the glory of the game.

|||||||||||||

In the years following Owen's death, his friends gave their own testimony about his friendship on the "RIP Owen Thomas" Facebook page. Although tributes would come from many who knew him—and even from acquaintances he'd known casually—the page clearly became a place where men who were part of the brotherhood of football players at Parkland and at Penn came to remember the fallen warrior. Many would address Owen directly on the page, as if there were a direct line to Valhalla.

Some wrote briefly, their few words still poignant. Penn housemate and Quakers teammate Adam Triglia would simply state, "Miss you, brother."

Andy Roth, whom Owen continued to recognize as part of the brotherhood even after he left Parkland football, shared a photo of his motorcycle, emblazoned with number 31—Owen's Parkland jersey number. Andy would return to the page again each time the artwork on the cycle was refurbished. Another photo showed an elaborate tattoo with Owen's initials, a heart, his high school football number 31, and angel wings stretching across the shoulder blades of former Parkland teammate Erik Rueda. "You will ALWAYS have my back FOREVER. . . . Miss you my brother I love you and miss you so much every day," he wrote.

For many, posting online was a way to process their grief—a space they would return to each April on the anniversary of his passing or on any day when he came to mind.

Mike Fay used the page to talk about the end of one of the most significant friendships of his life. He wrote, "I was just watching some videos today of me and OT in the past and it just reminded me how much my life revolved around him . . . it was subtle, but Owen was a major crutch in my life . . . he helped me stand. I felt my heart ripped out when I watched his big smile all over my video camera but in the end all I could do was smile, look up, and say 'we win.' I'm not sure why those words came out of my mouth at that moment but I'm pretty sure it was because I finally realized that Owen's death was not a defeat . . . it could not be a defeat, because we had already won long ago."

At the start of college football season, Owen's older brother Matt came to the page to reminisce about watching the start of college football season together on the television in their parents' basement. "Miss you, little brother," he'd write.

The passage of time slowed the number of notes posted, but it did not stop them. One social media post about Owen even went viral. Justin Reilly, the spoken-word poet from Penn's Excelano Project who had performed a poem in Owen's honor at the memorial on the Penn campus, posted a YouTube video of himself reciting it. A year after Owen's death, he reported that the video had been seen on four continents and been shared from two thousand Facebook and Twitter accounts and three hundred blogs and websites, amassing six thousand unique views. Reilly wrote, "The popularity is a testament to the love that so many people have for you. You touched so many people in your short time on this earth."

CHAPTER 11

DIVINE PROVIDENCE

ON A SUMMER SUNDAY a year after Owen's death, members of Union United Church of Christ arrived to find a camera crew hovering inside the red-carpeted vestibule of the church. A microphone on the end of a boom was ready to insinuate itself, giraffe-like, into the center aisle to capture the service.

Filmmakers looking for a location might well choose the church. It has an almost storybook feel, an appearance that one associates with classic Americana. Its simple redbrick exterior is topped with a pristine white steeple. A bell chimes the hours throughout the day, the melodies overriding traffic noise as they float over surrounding fields and suburban housing developments. A grove flanking one of the church parking lots is dotted with mature trees. A playground sits adjacent to a refreshment stand. To the rear of the building, a graveyard stretches for several acres. Its tombstones, some dating back nearly a hundred years, chronicle the generations of families who attended Union UCC. Tom Thomas, having served as pastor for more than a quarter century, will be buried there with his family. That spring, Owen became the first in the family laid to rest.

The crew, arriving on a summer weekend to shoot a documentary based on Chris Nowinski's book, *Head Games*, was happy, no doubt, about the semi-rustic locale. Owen was not part of Nowinski's book about concussions and young athletes. When it was published in 2006, he was still in high school playing for the Parkland Trojans. Indeed, the book predated Nowinski's founding of the Concussion Legacy Foundation and the establishment of the CTE brain bank at Boston University. Owen's death and subsequent CTE diagnosis had made his story an important segment in the documentary.

Attendance was light the day the film crew arrived—typical of summer Sundays. Pastor Tom took his place in front of the assemblage in his white robe topped by a green stole and intoned the United Church of Christ's signature greeting: "No matter who you are or where you are on life's journey—"

"—you are welcome here," the congregation responded.

Tom began making the weekly announcements that typically preceded the service: news of fundraisers, the church picnic, the summer sale of vegetables benefiting local food banks. That morning, there was an unusual note: "You may notice a film crew here during worship today," Pastor Tom said in his soft baritone. "They are here making a documentary that will include my son Owen."

When the documentary *Head Games* was eventually released in 2012, members of Union United Church of Christ saw a scene that captured that typical Sunday morning. A long shot showed the congregation singing the opening hymn before cutting to organist Blake Hoppes at the keyboard. There was a close-up of the mural of Christ being taken down from the cross that dominates the altar. Finally, there was a close-up of Tom Thomas in profile, his words that Sunday morning proving to be the perfect transition to Owen's story.

"There is a concept of divine providence," Pastor Tom said to the congregation. "Some of us deal with disease, illness, hardship, or heartache. We grieve the loss of those we have loved."

As Tom spoke, the visual transitioned to a framed triptych of photos of Owen that hangs in the Thomases' house. In them, he is forever the young man with silky, shoulder-length red hair and piercing blue eyes. He is forever no older than twenty-one.

The documentary recounts his athletic career, death, and subsequent CTE diagnosis in a ten-minute segment. It includes interviews with his parents, his brother Morgan, Parkland High School's athletics director Jeffrey Geisel, and University of Pennsylvania athletic trainer Eric Laudano. Perhaps the most striking utterance in the documentary comes from Morgan, who says, "Owen and I were similar in this aspect: If we did have a live head ringer, we would not go report that to the trainer. We would just shake it off and go back in there and play."

Interviewed in the film, awarding-winning journalist Alan Schwarz, a University of Pennsylvania alumnus who is credited with exposing the NFL's cover-up of head injuries, all but shouts at the camera as he stresses the importance of Owen's role in the unfolding story of concussions in sports.

"The Owen Thomas finding is not significant as it related to the cause of death," Schwarz says, his energy on camera palpable. "He could have died in a car accident and the significance of the finding would have been exactly the same. It would have been important to recognize, 'Holy Cow! CTE can actually begin before someone reaches the National Football League!'"

Schwarz's comment underscores how Owen's CTE diagnosis resonated in his circle of friends—the brotherhood of football boys with whom he'd played the game. The idea that football, the activity central to their lives, could have played a part in his death, was unfathomable. The unspoken question, seldom articulated, among all of them: "Could I have it too?"

John Zaccaro, who had been a linebacker with Owen on the Parkland Trojans, struggled to reconcile memories of the jarring impacts he himself had felt on the field with the thought that the same type of collisions may have contributed to his friend's death. Chronic traumatic encephalopathy had gone from being something that happened to a few old, dead pros in the NFL to a disease that had touched him in the most personal way. A handsome young man with short dark hair and liquid-brown eyes, John appeared suddenly older and a shadow fell across his face. He knew what it meant to "have your bell rung," the classic phrase players used to describe the aftermath of a hard hit.

"I mean, there were times when I definitely saw stars and been hit pretty hard. . . . You kind of feel like you're drunk. You kind of do. You feel like you don't know what the hell's going on. You're stumbling around out there—you're like, 'What?'" John deliberately slurs the last word, imitating the speech of someone who is inebriated. "It's different when you get your bell rung real good, but [it's not a concussion]. You quickly see a couple of little stars, and you shake it off. It's hard to explain. Maybe that *could* be just as bad. I don't know."

John shook his head, his eyes troubled.

"I'm not saying that it had nothing to do with [Owen's death]. I'm just saying." He paused, and when he spoke again, his bewilderment was apparent. "It was just such a shocker to us. Such a surprise to us. He was such a beast at football. *How could he die from football?* He was so good at it. How could it turn into that? He was extremely, extremely smart so . . . I don't know. He wouldn't be purposely leading with his head. He was smart in every aspect of his life. He was smart about the way he used his body. Know what I mean? He was smart about not taking unnecessary hits. Not leading with the top of his head. . . . It's just hard to believe."

Jamie Pagliaro, who'd played softball and football with Owen from elementary through high school, returned to play during his senior year at William & Mary. He was team captain, just as Owen would have been at Penn if he had lived. "I tried to do what he did at Parkland. And what I know he would have done at Penn that last year," Pags said. "Be the voice and let them know that you are going to follow them into battle." He paused. "I dedicated that year to Owen."

Owen became a kind of guardian angel over Pags's last season of play, a spirit he called upon for help. "I remember we were playing the number one team in the nation, Delaware, and their kicker comes up to kick the field goal. We were up by two, my buddy was looking at me and said, 'We need to block arms.' I said, 'Hold on,' and I said, 'Owen, please make him miss this field goal.' He kicked it and missed it. We won the game."

Jamie grinned and suddenly, his face softened.

"I felt him. He was always there with me."

Marc Quilling entered his senior year at Lafayette College wearing a black rubber wristband with red letters: RIP Owen Thomas. He'd had the bands made as part of a fundraiser to support erecting a special tombstone for Owen. He was wearing it when he found himself playing for the Lafayette Leopards at the Penn Quakers 2010 home opener. Although he was not named starting quarterback for his last college season, an injury to the starter in the Leopards' first game placed Marc in the lineup against Penn. It meant he'd be quarterback at a game where the opposing team would remember his dead friend with a moment of silence before the kickoff at Franklin Field.

"The week leading up to the game, I tried to mentally prepare myself, knowing they would do something to honor him—even talking with my head coach and position coach one-on-one in their offices," Marc said. "Before the game, emotions were high and they did a video tribute and moment of silence during which I couldn't really hold it together."

He paused, his voice almost hoarse with sadness. "I can honestly say that was the only game of my life when I wasn't mentally all in. There were too many thoughts and emotions running through my head. I was wishing I was playing against my best friend, with his red hair hanging out of the back of his helmet. I ended up playing my worst game ever, but it was also against an extremely strong, motivated team," Marc said.

Suddenly, his tone is bemused. "Thinking back, if he was there, it probably would've been an even worse game for me, due to him trash talking me and trying to take off my head. I would've never heard the end of it."

It was an equally challenging game for the Quakers. An ESPN crew had prepared a segment about the team honoring their late teammate, number 40, Owen Thomas. The piece, airing on Saturday morning before the Lafayette game, included interviews with team members, coaches, and Owen's father, Tom. In his on-camera interview, Tom said haltingly, "I pray for the strength to be a survivor." The segment provided an extra push for a team that had already decided to dedicate its season to Owen and to its eighty-five-year-old "spirit coach" Dan "Lake" Staffierri, the team's unofficial cheerleader for decades. The two had died within weeks of each other. At that first game, the Quakers scored a 19–14 victory over the Leopards.

In the postgame press conference after the season opener, recorded by Penn's student newspaper, the *Daily Pennsylvanian*, a woman—never seen on camera—identified herself as a French reporter and asked Coach Al Bagnoli about the announcement of Owen's CTE diagnosis. The announcement had come just five days before the game. Chuckling slightly, Bagnoli said, "None of us knew that they had requested his brain to be tested. So when it came out, we were caught a little off guard. Didn't have much notice in terms of trying to notify our kids and everything." Noting that the announcement came on a Monday, the team's day off, Bagnoli said they had scrambled to notify the players using email and text messaging. "Obviously, it's something we need to pay attention to but I don't think it affects the way we play or the way we practice."[1]

The off-camera reporter next questioned the two players sitting with Bagnoli, senior cornerback Jon Saelinger and sophomore quarterback Billy Ragone. "And you guys: are you afraid? Do you think of that?" she said in her heavy Gallic accent. Saelinger responded first. "I heard the news and I don't really think about it when I'm on the field. My mom heard about it and said something to me and was concerned. I've played football most of my life and it's not something you can really think about when you're out there," he said.

The camera panned to Ragone. "It was shocking news to everyone that that was kind of a factor in what had happened to Owen but, just like Jon said, we've been playing this game since we were young. It's second nature now and once you step on the field, nothing else enters your mind," Ragone said.[2]

Behind the scenes, not all of the Quakers were as calm in the aftermath of their friend's death. None were more profoundly affected than the roommates from Baltimore Avenue, who had moved to a new house for their senior year—without Owen. Dave Macknet found the fall 2010 football season like no other in more than a decade playing the game. "I started playing when I was eight," Dave said. "The scariest time I ever had playing football was the season after Owen passed away. Justin [Cosgrove] really struggled with this too. The fact Owen had this diagnosis of CTE made you question every hit you take, every hit you make. I was able to push that aside eventually but I had to take some time off during practice just to think about it."

Macknet and other teammates, who were eventually able to move past it, said it was more difficult for Justin, who had found Owen's body. He remained deeply shaken when the Penn football team returned for fall practice.

"He definitely carried a burden with him that none of us can know the severity of," Dave said. "I wish we could carry that burden. Justin, like Owen, is such a great guy. That memory that he carries—that he had to cut Owen down and perform CPR. I wish we could take that burden from him."

Jake Peterson recalled that Justin switched numbers so he would no longer be in the same part of the locker room that he once shared with Owen. "I tried to talk to him some about life after death and this somehow being part of a plan, but Justin doesn't have those beliefs. It was a very difficult time for him," Jake said.

For Jake, an aggressive player, Owen's CTE diagnosis was a wake-up call. "When Owen passed, that changed the conversation. It made people a little more aware. Here's a young, healthy, great guy and he was never diagnosed with a concussion. And he could develop this," Jake said. "I used my head as a weapon for seventeen years. They gave me a helmet, so I was protected and I would try to inflict as much damage as I could. I couldn't do that anymore. If I hadn't already started to develop [CTE], I was on a one-way track. It was only a matter of time."

During his senior season at Penn, the fall after Owen died, Jake was occasionally troubled by suicidal thoughts that, in retrospect, he attributes to head trauma. "I was close to that ledge. I see what happened from Owen doing it," Jake said. "Those thoughts weren't me. I had no reason for that. I had an awesome life. Things were great. In hindsight, I'm able to identify emotions, the thoughts I was experiencing, as symptoms of brain trauma."

That same season, the Quakers won their second consecutive All-Ivy title. The loss of Owen had heightened their resolve, and their intensity was reminiscent of their earliest days on the gridiron, when they played for the love of the game and their teammates.

"That was the closest team I've ever been on," Jake said. "It was the most unified, the most close-knit. I think that was the biggest contributing factor. From seniors to freshmen, all of us were close. You don't get that in a college program, with that many kids. That was saying a lot. I loved the team. The head coach and myself did not get along very well. Bagnoli and I had a volatile relationship. But I stayed because of the guys. Because we were close."

Some friends rejected the idea that CTE caused or contributed to Owen's death. Mike Fay insisted that the suicide was the reaction of someone who had never faced failure before. His friend—always top of the class and the star on the playing field—was struggling at school, Mike said. Noting that his older brother, Anthony, had labored for six years to make it through Wharton while playing football, he blamed academic pressure, not the sport, for Owen's death.

"The best people in the world go to Wharton," Mike said. "Going there, he met his match and his match was kicking his ass."

He emphasized Owen never had a diagnosed concussion. "Can you get it without concussions?" he said, a note of challenge in his voice. "He never had concussions."

CTE researchers, over time, would answer the question that Mike posed. In 2018, researchers led by Dr. Lee Goldstein, associate professor at Boston University School of Medicine and College of Engineering, published a study that showed that it was jarring impacts to the head known as subconcussive hits—not merely concussions—that were the precursors to CTE. The study, which took seven years, involved researchers from Boston University, Cleveland Clinic, Harvard Medical School, Lawrence Livermore National Laboratory, Ben-Gurion University of the Negev, and Oxford University.

The research first looked at the brains of deceased teens and young adults who recently had sustained mild head trauma, but who had died of other causes. Researchers found early evidence of brain damage consistent with CTE. It included the buildup of tau protein synonymous with the condition. In the second phase of their study, the researchers used laboratory mice in experiments that exposed them to head impacts like those in sports or military blast exposure. What they saw in the animals was early evidence of the damage associated with CTE. Even a small amount of trauma produced it.[3]

The research confirmed what Ann McKee and those at the Concussion Legacy Foundation believed: Owen's was a landmark case, one that suggested that you didn't need a concussion to cause the disease. Enduring more than a decade of jarring hits that started in childhood, his brain had moved in his skull like an amusement park bumper car. The game had left the muddy fingerprints of the disease indelibly on his brain.

CHAPTER 12

CHANGING
THEIR MINDS

ANN MCKEE HAD SIGNED ON to do research at Boston University's CTE Center, but as its director she was increasingly the public face of the issue of head trauma in football. A meticulous researcher who was used to presenting results to medical colleagues who recognized her acumen, McKee was at first unprepared for criticism that was based not on dispassionate science but on emotional or financial ties to a sport that was a central part of American culture. It was an especially difficult position for someone brought up as a football fan but trained as a scientist.

"I talk to people who respect me, who I consider very close friends, and then they finish the conversation, say what great work I'm doing, and then they're promoting football," McKee says. "It's almost like we have a disconnect. . . . I mean, I notice it even in my family. My family gets it, but they don't really get it. You know, that football could be very dangerous to your health."

With each new case coming under her microscope, McKee knew that playing football was causing irreversible brain damage. As her research progressed, she was in constant demand with the news media, juggling interviews between clinical and research responsibilities. Some days would find her wondering aloud, as yet another journalist was ushered into her office, whether this was the reporter from *Sports Illustrated* or the person writing a book. "I don't think a lot about the public attention. I enjoy the interviews because I enjoy talking about the patients and their families and I enjoy talking about the work. . . . The work is fascinating to me so I enjoy talking about it," she said. "I'm a teacher at heart, so I feel like instead of teaching medical students, I teach the public."

McKee turned down few interviews or speaking requests, leading to a round-the-clock work schedule that left little time for sleep. Painting, still a passion in her off hours, is relegated to a few hours on the weekends. She packs her paints to take on business trips, but seldom gets to use them. Colleagues, receiving emails with a 4 a.m. time stamp, express concern about a schedule that leads to long days and longer nights.

Dr. Michael Alosco is an assistant professor of neurology at Boston University School of Medicine and a member of McKee's team at the CTE Center, where he conducts clinical interviews with family members and other caregivers of deceased athletes whose brains have been donated to the center. McKee has mentored him since he first joined the university as a postdoctoral fellow. Although he praises her for being generous with her time, he also has urged her to slow down. "She'll travel across the country and even the world to do these smaller scale events and conferences. She doesn't say no to anything. She says yes to everything. Even a fifteen- or twenty-person conference. I'll say, 'Ann, you don't have to do that,'" Alosco says.

But the speaking and interview requests are still secondary compared to another aspect of her job: speaking with the families of deceased athletes whose brains were analyzed in her lab. McKee is as committed to the calls with the families as she is to her research. Without the brains, there is no research.

After she and her research team at the Boston University CTE Center finish analyzing a brain, they review their findings in a phone call with the family of the deceased athlete. In 2010, one of the phone calls was with Kathy Brearley and Tom Thomas, telling them that Owen had CTE.

The families always remember the phone call.

It can provide the answer to the question of why family members saw personality changes, memory loss, angry outbursts, problems with impulse control, and more in their loved one. It explains why the person they lost seemed to disappear, even before he died.

The number of confirmed CTE cases was in the twenties at the time of Owen's death. As the years went by and the number of brains donated to research moved from double to triple digits, some of McKee's colleagues questioned the hours she spends on the phone with families. It takes time away from her research.

"I think it's very important. I feel very honored that they've donated the brain," McKee says. "I feel very privileged that I'm allowed this insight into their life that others may not have. . . . I consider it very private information, very—I don't have any other words for it. It's private. It's personal."

She likes being able to answer the family's questions—except for the inevitable question that she can't answer.

"Why did he commit suicide?"

"You know, that's the number one [question] that I don't have an answer for," she says, with a touch of sadness in her voice. Although she can confirm that brain trauma can cause depression and impulsivity, the exact sequence of events leading to the act of suicide is complex, unique to each individual's circumstances.

The phone calls are exhausting. They can go on for an hour or more. McKee stays on the line as long as the family needs to talk, answering questions and listening. "It almost turns into a mini therapy session," Michael Alosco says.

The families remember the way that McKee made them feel. Lisa McHale, the wife of Tom McHale, whose groundbreaking case was announced at the 2009 Super Bowl, put it simply: "She gave me back my Prince Charming." McKee had offered the explanation for her late husband's changed behavior.[1] "Maybe what's unexpected with families is her level of empathy," says Chris Nowinski. "She cares, and you can tell. And she feels the pain of families, and you can tell."

Years into the research, after dozens of brains have been analyzed, Nowinski says McKee has exceeded any expectations he had when he hired her to direct the CTE Center. "She sympathizes and empathizes with her donors. And that always comes out in her interviews, and it comes out in private conversations we have with families. And they can tell she's committed."

Families' appreciation for McKee was apparent when Nowinski's Concussion Legacy Foundation honored her in 2011 with its Impact Award for research showing a link between CTE and amyotrophic lateral sclerosis—also known as ALS, or Lou Gehrig's disease. As McKee made her way to the podium to receive the award, people lined up to hug her.[2]

The 2011 recognition, while gratifying, did not reflect the opinions of some in the larger research community. When the paper linking the two conditions was first published in 2010 in the *Journal of Neuropathology and Experimental Neurology*, McKee says, "We got a lot of pushback on that."

It's the kind of reaction to her work that McKee would see time and again during the decade after Owen Thomas's death. Sometimes the words she chooses to describe the negative reactions from the scientific and sports communities are more colorful than "pushback."

"People really think I'm off my rocker," she says in a moment of frustration, straightforward in characterizing the many criticisms of her work. A moment later, she tempers it. "But they're changing their minds."

Changing their minds would come with the slow unfolding of more and more CTE research from McKee and her colleagues. Their first challenge was getting the medical and research communities to agree that CTE was a disease, distinct from other neurodegenerative conditions like Alzheimer's disease. McKee never wavered in her confidence about her findings.

"At the time of Owen Thomas, I knew this was a disease. I knew this was a problem, and then we just kept getting more and more cases. . . . And there was a time period where I was certainly saying to myself, 'Just wait. Just wait. OK, you don't believe me now, but you will. It's just a matter of time,'" she remembers. "I'm hearing all this opposition, I'm hearing all the criticisms, but you're not sitting where I'm sitting. I'm sitting in a strange spot with a different perspective and this disease isn't going away and this disease is not rare."

There would be milestones in the research that answered criticisms from those who could not accept that football caused a distinct traumatic brain injury.

A 2013 paper spelled out criteria for diagnosing CTE and established definitions for four stages of the disease. One of the most important aspects of the paper, McKee says, is that it assessed, for the first time, the number of years a person had played football. "We found that there was a direct correlation between the number of years you played football and the grade or the severity of the CTE. So that was our first inkling of a dose response," McKee says. Playing for a longer period of time, sustaining more hits, was common among those diagnosed with a higher stage of the disease.

Continued resistance to the idea of CTE as a distinct disease with its own diagnostic criteria was addressed again when the researchers used a National Institutes of Health grant in 2015 to convene what they called "a consensus conference of experts." They brought together expert neuropathologists and gave them seven hundred slides representing twenty-five cases. Some had CTE and others had different conditions—including an extremely rare type of dementia that exists only on the island of Guam. Using the criteria for diagnosing CTE established in the 2013 paper, the experts were charged with evaluating the cases. "We gave them the slides, and over 90 percent of the time, they could tell CTE from all these other diseases," McKee says.

Despite such evidence, resistance did not go away. In addition to questioning whether CTE was a disease, critics from the research community, the NFL, and even fans of the sport continued to resist linking it to playing football. Little wonder, since football's popularity remained high. Super Bowls from 2009 through 2019 have ranked as the ten most-watched games since the contest started, and the past eight were the most-watched programs in US television history. The 2020 game continued the trend. Any decrease in television viewership was offset by those watching it via online streaming.[3]

For Ann McKee, passionately committed to her research, this meant listening to people, sometimes even other researchers, accuse her of "bad science." Over and over again, her research would be criticized for "selection bias," a term that refers to the fact that the brains were donated by players or family members who suspected that symptoms and behavior might indicate the presence of CTE. McKee always openly acknowledged this bias.

The importance of the research helped her to keep the criticism in perspective. "You have to develop a sort of callousness," she says. "You have to think, 'I can't control, I have no control of what you think about me, but I know what I think is important so I'm just going to keep going.'"

Although playing football and watching football was not going away, the expanding body of CTE research began to make an impact, reflected in more rule changes in all levels of the sport.

New concussion protocols designed by the NFL's Head, Neck and Spine Committee were released in 2013. The protocols included a symptom checklist, a limited neurological examination that included a cognitive evaluation, and a balance assessment.[4] That same year, a new rule imposed a fifteen-yard penalty on players making a crown-of-the-helmet hit outside the tackle box. The rule, the league said, was meant to protect both the player receiving the hit and the player delivering it.[5] The concussion protocols would be updated in 2017 and included rules requiring follow-up evaluations for players on the day after a game. The updated protocols also required examination of players who fell to the ground or were unable to stand for nonorthopedic injuries.[6]

Perhaps the most significant milestone would be the $765-million concussion settlement with former players, announced just before the start of the 2013 NFL season. It outlined maximum benefits for various neurological conditions: $3 million for dementia, $4 million for CTE, and $5 million for ALS. With a lengthy required application and review process, it would be years before the first players would receive money from the settlement.[7] In reporting on the settlement, *The Guardian* newspaper pointed out that the NFL admitted no wrongdoing, saying the settlement "states clearly that, despite making these payments, they are not accepting liability or admitting that the plaintiffs' injuries were caused by football."[8] The first two awards totaling $9 million would not be announced until 2017.[9]

In 2011, news on the college level began to reflect the impact of Owen's death. The Ivy League announced it would limit full-contact practices to twice weekly with the start of the season. The change exceeded NCAA guidelines, which at the time set the limit at five. The new rules also limited Ivy League teams to two full-pads practices a day during summer "two-a-days," and reduced the number of full-contact practices during spring training.[10] Al Bagnoli, the head coach at Penn under whom Owen had played, was part of the committee making the recommendation. Interviewed by WHYY, Philadelphia's National Public Radio affiliate, he acknowledged Owen's death played a role in the league's decision.[11] In 2016,

Ivy League teams would completely eliminate full-contact hitting during practice.[12]

However, the NCAA would lag behind in setting limits on full-contact practices in which players tackle. Following a 2016 Safety in College Football Summit, the organization would end the tradition of two-a-day full contact practices in preseason, citing evidence that a high number of concussions occur in practices.[13]

By January 2016, college athletes would have a concussion settlement of their own. The ruling followed a 2011 lawsuit brought by a former Eastern Illinois University football player, Adrian Arrington. The initial settlement was amended in 2019. The NCAA set up a fifty-year medical monitoring program to screen and track concussions paid for by a $70 million medical monitoring fund. According to the law firm Hagens Berman Sobol Shapiro, which represented student athletes in a class-action lawsuit, the amended settlement also included significant changes to the NCAA's concussion management policies and return-to-play guidelines. It established that all players receive a seasonal, baseline test to better assess concussions sustained during the season. Those sustaining a concussion would need to be cleared before returning to play. The settlement also stipulated that a medical professional trained in diagnosing concussions will be present at all contact-sport games and it established reporting mandates for concussions and treatment. The NCAA also agreed to supply $5 million for concussion research. The settlement did not cover medical costs, however; it paid only for testing and diagnosis.

Almost as soon as the original 2016 settlement was announced, players from Penn State, Auburn, Georgia, Oregon, Utah, and Vanderbilt universities filed class action lawsuits against their conferences and former schools over how their concussions were treated.[14] By early 2019, more than three hundred suits had been filed against the NCAA by former players claiming their concussions were not treated properly.[15]

In March 2016, there appeared to be a sense that the NFL was beginning to acknowledge growing evidence about the link between head trauma and playing football. In a roundtable on Capitol Hill, Jeff Miller, the league's senior vice president for health and safety policy, responded to a pointed question from Representative Jan Schakowsky, an Illinois Democrat, whether "there is a link between football and degenerative brain disorders like CTE." Hesitantly, Miller said yes, that Dr. Ann McKee and her colleagues had found the disease in many deceased players. But, he added, it was still to be determined how prevalent the disease is among former players.[16] Miller would leave his position with the NFL later that year.

In the lab, McKee and other researchers continued their relentless pursuit of answers that could solve a conundrum key to the CTE mystery: how to diagnose the disease before patients die. A 2017 study published by McKee and her colleagues showed that the answer might be a protein associated with inflammation in the brain called CCL11. The researchers believe the protein, found circulating in spinal fluid, could be measured to show the presence of CTE in patients' brains. Because proteins in spinal fluid are known to make their way into the bloodstream, CCL11 could help researchers to develop a blood test that could tell patients if they have the beginnings of the disease. The information could be used by younger athletes to determine when it's time to curtail playing or stop taking heavy hits.[17]

McKee and her team had found that the levels of the CCL11 protein rose in proportion to the number of years that former athletes with CTE had played. The levels were highest among former pro players who had played sixteen years or more.[18]

Meanwhile, in November 2017, another breakthrough was announced. Dr. Julian Bailes, neurosurgeon and codirector of NorthShore University HealthSystem in Evanston, Illinois, published findings in the journal *Neurosurgery* that a brain scan of an NFL veteran had revealed the presence of CTE four years before his death. An autopsy conducted after he died confirmed that what was seen on the scan proved to be an accurate indicator of the disease.

But none of these findings would catch the attention of the media and the public the way a paper published in July 2017 in the *Journal of the American Medical Association* by McKee and her team did. Its findings would be reported by media worldwide, with online searches of media coverage reaching 989,000 hits.

The study reported that out of 202 deceased football players studied by McKee and her colleagues, a majority—87 percent—were found to have CTE. The paper confirmed that 110 of 111 brains of former NFL players, and 48 of 51 brains of college players, were found to have the disease. Owen Thomas was one of them. In addition, the paper affirmed a link between the length of time a man played football and his having CTE: the longer someone played the sport, the more likely he was to have the disease. The study found something important to the family and friends of Owen Thomas: even those with mild cases exhibited cognitive, mood, and behavioral symptoms, such as depression and memory problems and fits of anger.

Although the opportunity to raise public awareness was valuable, McKee is cautious about the media attention. "Ninety-nine percent of NFL players don't get CTE, and we said that many times in the paper. But the media stormed Twitter, everything," she says.

After years of criticism, the reaction was gratifying. "For the most part, it changed the psyche of the American public. There was something about that paper, and I certainly wouldn't have appreciated that or foreseen that, but I think that paper turned the public appreciation that this is a disease, or this is something to be reckoned with. It's not imaginary. It's a problem."

McKee adds that the torrent of media attention for the study had another benefit: it prompted more parents to start to think about the risks of allowing their children to play football. Both McKee and Nowinski draw a distinction between professional players and youth football.

"Grown men doing something to their bodies is one thing, but there's thousands of kids that emulate them," McKee says. "And those kids want to be and act just like those guys, and for them, the dangers are higher and they're dealing with coaches that aren't always very informed."

Youth football has followed the pros and colleges in rule changes to increase player safety. For example, in 2016, Pop Warner, the nation's oldest youth football program, eliminated kickoffs, considered one of the sport's most dangerous plays, in its three youngest age divisions. It also reduced the amount of contact time allowed in practice from 33 percent to 25 percent.[19] Youth football's governing body, USA Football, established guidelines limiting contact to 30 minutes per practice, 120 minutes per week preseason, and 90 minutes in season.[20]

Despite such changes, it appears that concerns about traumatic brain injury are reducing participation in youth football. The number of youth between the ages of six and seventeen participating in tackle football dropped from 6.7 million in 2009 to 5.2 million in 2018.[21] Participation in eleven-man high school football dropped more than 10 percent between 2009 and 2018. Even states with long-established traditions of sending players to college teams and to the NFL have seen drops. For example, Texas saw a 10 percent decrease on the high school level, while participation on high school teams in Ohio plummeted 27 percent.[22]

There was another significant change. In 2006, more than 75 percent of high school players were white. That figure had dropped to 56 percent by 2018. A New York Times analysis reported that in 2006 nearly 70 percent of high school football players whose parents did not have a college degree were white. By 2018, that number was 30 percent. Among African Americans, the number in that category was just under 20 percent in 2006. By 2018, that number had doubled, with more than 40 percent of African American players falling in that category.[23]

Such figures reflect something that is a concern for many: as more middle-class white families abandon football because of concerns about head injuries, it may increasingly become a game for lower-income minority families who see it as a way for their sons to earn college scholarships. The racial disparity was underscored in a *New York Times* story about the one hundredth anniversary of the NFL that reported that roughly 74 percent of the league's players are black.[24]

The changes on all levels of the sport prompted the National Football Foundation, a nonprofit organization that promotes amateur football's ability to develop scholarship, citizenship, and athletic achievement among young players, to launch the Football Matters campaign with an eye on rebranding the sport in a more positive light. The foundation also sponsors the College Football Hall of Fame. There is a Football Matters website with information for parents about rule changes and improved safety in the sport and facts promoting the academic success of players. The hashtags #FootballMatters and #UnitedWeFan link to social media posts and YouTube videos that celebrate the positive experiences of being a member of a team, capture the color of high school games, and promote players and coaches giving back to the community.[25]

Despite declines, football remains the most popular sport for young athletes, with about 1.1 million high school players in the United States in 2019.[26] With the pervasiveness of football in American culture, Chris Nowinski knows that more needs to be done to educate parents on the dangers of allowing kids to play football when they are too young. In addition to its efforts to build voluntary donations of brains for further research, the Concussion Legacy Foundation places much of its focus on reducing first-time participation. Once boys are already playing, the ties to the brotherhood they share with other boys is more powerful than the appeal of the sport itself.

"Parents don't look at it as taking their kid out of football. Parents look at it as taking their son away from their friends.

And so, we don't even strategically target the parents whose kids are already in football, to change their mind. Because, we've shown that that's virtually impossible. We target the parents who are choosing whether or not to put their kid in for the first time next year," Nowinski says.

For some, the evidence from McKee's research will not be enough to shake ties to a sport that he says has been mythologized in American culture more than any other sport. "Part of it is, what is stronger than science, is emotion," Nowinski says.

CHAPTER 13

BUT NOT FORGOTTEN

TOM THOMAS STANDS waiting under a tree in his white ministerial robe, an ivory satin stole trimmed in red and gold draped around his neck. The tree, ancient and imposing, has been transformed into the altar of an outdoor chapel. As its leaves rustle overhead, an antique chandelier and a graceful swath of white cloth wound through the branches sway with the breeze, drawing a bemused smile from the minister. Church pews are lined up on the lawn in front of Pastor Tom, filled with guests waiting for the wedding party to arrive on a Saturday in May 2015.

Tom glances at his wife, Kathy, seated among the crowd. Her face is composed, almost serene. Just a week earlier, Tom had admitted that this wedding—and the rehearsal dinner the night before—would be difficult for him. Marc Quilling, Owen's teammate since childhood, was marrying Brittni Kitaen Evans. The couple had asked him to do the honors, formalizing the union that was affirmed three years before with the birth of their son, Chase Owen. Tom would never refuse Marc's request, but the might-have-beens are heartbreaking as he presides at the wedding of one of his son's closest friends.

In a way, Owen had a hand in introducing the bride and groom. Marc and Brittni first met when they were out partying at a favorite bar with friends. She'd noted that the handsome guy who'd caught her eye was wearing dog tags. Was he a military man? she'd asked flirtatiously, fingering the tags. Turning suddenly serious, Marc explained that he'd had them made in memory of a friend who had died. The larger tag boasted a black matte background engraved with Owen's initials—O.D.B.T.— and the dates 9/30/88–4/26/10. The smaller silver tag bore the title of the Led Zeppelin song "Over the Hills and Far Away." Brittni would later say that the emotion he'd displayed at that moment convinced her that he was special.

Just three weeks before the wedding, Tom and Kathy marked the fifth anniversary of Owen's death. On that day, just as she had every April 26, Kathy had placed a memorial ad in the local newspaper, *The Morning Call*. That year, she'd noted in the memoriam that Owen would be the angel watching over his buddy Quill's wedding.

The anniversary was especially painful for Marc, making him keenly aware that one of his closest friends would not be with him on his wedding day. "It was a tough couple of days," he said. He made a decision. He would wear one of Owen's old T-shirts under his tux so that his friend would be with him. Stashed under his bed in plastic boxes, Marc keeps a collection of T-shirts from his football days. There's the red and gray one from Parkland football, proclaiming "We survived double sessions together—2002," on the front, with the word "Team" on the back. Or the one from their freshman year that proclaimed, "Freshmen Undefeated 2003," followed by the boast "Us: 366, Them: 36, 7 Shut Outs." Although both of those shirts carried memories inextricably associated with Owen, they were not the one he chose. He picked the one displaying the word Buffaloes in red on a dark gray shirt. The Thomases had given it to him as a memento. It was one of Owen's old North Parkland youth league tees, signifying the beginning of their friendship when they had met playing baseball and football. That was the one he wore beneath his shirt on his wedding day.

Before the ceremony Marc and his groomsmen gathered in one of the farm's buildings to dress. There were familiar faces from Parkland football days. Mike Fay, Jamie Pagliaro, Chris Funk; all of them were part of the wedding party. Also, four of Marc's teammates from Lafayette College were groomsmen, along with Brittni's younger brother, Evan. Marc's brother, Ryan, was best man. They took turns helping each other fasten suspenders, button shirt cuffs, and pin on boutonnieres, hoisting a few beers as they prepared. At one point, a bottle of Jack Daniels made the rounds among them. Someone had brought a football—an unlikely addition to wedding preparations, perhaps, but for the group it was a touchstone, the symbol of what had cemented their friendships for so many years.

The ball came in handy as a distraction for tiny Chase Owen, Marc and Brittni's son. In between donning their wedding gear, the men took turns holding the ball for the toddler as he attempted a punt. Finally, he sent the ball flying to the delight of the men who once played the game. Soon Marc's father lent a hand to help dress the little boy in a facsimile of the adult tuxedos: black pants, shirt, and shoes.

When the time came for the ceremony, Marc and the groomsmen formed a line in front of the guests, facing front in anticipation of the bride's entrance. Coming down a path strewn with rose petals, nine bridesmaids walked with deliberate, measured steps, their long, soft gray dresses brushing the blades of grass. Behind them, Brittni entered on her father's arm, her long black, three-quarter-length gloves dramatic against her white dress, a large bouquet of pink and white peonies clasped in her hand. To the east, a bank of dark clouds gathered, heralding a spring thunderstorm.

Brittni and Marc faced each other to make their vows, looking toward a shared future. They exchanged rings. They kissed. And then the couple exited past the rows of guests who tossed red rose petals, the wedding party streaming after them.

The clouds were more pronounced now and everyone wondered if the rain would hold off until the photos were taken. They seemed to grow more ominous with every click of the lens—the bride and groom with each family, the bride with her bridesmaids, the groom with his groomsmen, and, finally, the entire wedding party in formal poses and clowning around. Then, with the sky growing darker and darker, the wedding party made their entrance into the building where the reception was being held. The wind picked up as each couple was announced—until finally Marc and Brittni's entrance was signaled by the DJ's announcement: "Mr. and Mrs. Marc Quilling." They glided in, Brittni's bouquet of peonies held aloft like a torch. And then, to punctuate the moment, thunder rumbled and rain poured from the sky in sheets.

Mike Fay looked at Chris Funk. "Owen," he said. He's sure, through some otherworldly intercession, that their friend held the rain at bay.

Over the next few years, Tom would officiate at several weddings for the football boys, his dutiful attempt to fill the space left empty by his son. A year after the Quilling wedding, Emily Toth married Luke DeLuca, Owen's Penn roommate. Once again in an idyllic setting—this time a vineyard—the couple stood in front of Owen's father and became husband and wife. Once again, the palpable sense of loss was felt. And once again, as wedding pictures were taken, a storm gathered. In one shot, Luke dips Emily back for a dramatic kiss against the backdrop of ominously black clouds. As the shutter clicked, a bolt of lightning flashed overhead, forming a backdrop for their embrace. Owen again, some of them said.

In November 2016, at what would be the last wedding where Tom would officiate for one of Owen's former teammates, Mike Fay and his fiancée, Stephanie, were married. At the reception, the group inevitably reminisced about Owen. This time the talk turned to the time when Mike's car became stuck during a snowstorm.

"So, Mr. Thomas had to come out and get us." Mike pauses, reflecting on the memory—and remembering that Owen's father didn't share the story with Mike's parents, saving him a lecture about his carelessness. "We had a really good time."

During the reception, the stories are shared with light-hearted banter. But the day after the wedding, Kathy posted a wedding photo of the newlyweds on the "RIP Owen Thomas" page on Facebook, where she spoke to her dead son: "My heart breaks that you weren't there, again. Talked to all your friends who are now fine young men and women. Remembered the night you called us to pull Mike's car out of the snowy field. All the guys remembered it. Watch over Mike and Stephanie."

Although most of the young men have married, the game of football remains a constant in their lives. Former players have become enthusiastic fans, but a few remain actively involved in the sport as coaches. They follow the path of the men who coached them. Jamie Pagliaro's journey on the gridiron intersected once again with his Parkland coach, Jim Morgans, on the coaching staff of Allentown Central Catholic High School. On a fall Friday in 2019, both men are in Allentown's J. Birney Crum Stadium.

J. Birney Crum Stadium is a grand old sports venue, built in 1948 when rows of concrete stands rimmed with wood benches rose steeply from the track around the field. Now those benches are metal, and a 2002 renovation added a flashy new scoreboard—the Andre Reed scoreboard, named for the Allentown player who went on to play for the Buffalo Bills and Washington Redskins. Once the largest high school stadium in Pennsylvania, it is the home field for three schools—the city's public high schools, William Allen and Louis E. Dieruff, and Allentown Central Catholic. The stadium is surrounded by city neighborhoods that are overrun by drivers seeking parking on game nights. If residents on the streets around the stadium wonder who is playing, they need only listen to the booming public address system. If they hear the sound of a prayer being raised just before "The Star-Spangled Banner" is played, they know the Central Catholic Vikings are on the field tonight.

Inside the stadium on a cool October night, Central Catholic's cheerleaders are decked out in the school colors of green and gold, the word *Vikings* glittering on their shirts as they execute lifts and pyramids in front of the small but enthusiastic crowd. The loyalty of Central fans is evident, from the small boy and girl enthusiastically waving green and gold pom-poms to the middle-aged nun with the green and gold scarf wound around her neck, obviously prepared to spend the entire game standing in her sensible black shoes to cheer on her students playing on the field. It's Homecoming, and fans wearing shirts proclaiming "We Are Viking Nation—Homecoming 2019" are piling into the stands to watch their team take on Liberty High School's Hurricanes from nearby Bethlehem, Pennsylvania. Liberty's Grenadier Marching Band, famed for its bagpipe section decked out in plaid kilts, threatens to drown out everything else. The band's impressive size is a reminder that the much-smaller parochial school is facing off against one of the region's big public high schools. Central Catholic's fans don't seem concerned. Over the years, the high school has had its share of winning teams, including some that won conference and state championships against bigger schools. Quite a few of those winning teams were coached by Jim Morgans, who later went on to coach the Parkland Trojans.

Coach Morgans is in the stadium on this fall night, sitting with one of his daughters and a gaggle of his grandchildren high in the stands, at the very top where the stadium looks like it meets the sky. Morgans officially retired from coaching at Parkland in 2016, but in 2019, it was announced he'd be helping his alma mater, Central Catholic, as a consultant. And that is what he's doing at tonight's game: assessing the action, noting weaknesses, and sharing his expert opinion, honed during more than fifty years of playing and coaching football. That's why he's sitting far from the rest of the crowd: he's available for a quick conference next to the box where Central Catholic's head coach surveys the field. Although coaching has gone high tech, with drones giving coaches closeups of the action while plays are recorded on tablet computers on the sidelines, Morgans's experience still has value.

Coach Morgans ambles down one level in the stadium to chat with someone at halftime, and the conversation is interrupted more than once by people who know him: one of his daughters' friends, an old neighbor, or a former player. If it's a former player, there's likely to be a hug and an invitation to climb up to the top of the stadium in the second half to commiserate over the game. It's not surprising that Morgans hasn't fully retired. Football has been at the center of his life for more than half a century, and life without it seems empty. In May 2019, he was inducted into the Pennsylvania Scholastic Coaches Association Hall of Fame recognizing his years as one of the state's most successful coaches. The induction was the latest in more than a half-dozen halls of fame that have honored him. He's a member of the halls of fame at both Central Catholic and Parkland, as well as his college, Louisiana State. At retirement, his career record was 283–137–1. During his long career, his teams won two PIAA State Championships, two PIAA State Runner-ups, an Eastern Conference Title, ten East Penn Conference Titles, and eleven District XI Championships.[1]

Morgans talks about the way high school football is a game built on relationships—between players and coaches, among players on the team, and among the men who coach it. Over the years, as Morgans moved to various coaching jobs—twice at Central Catholic, twice at Parkland, and in shorter stints at a couple of other high schools—he brought coaching staff with him, or they followed him. That's why he always credited his staff—the ones who specialize in coaching the offensive or defensive line or special teams—for his success as head coach.

Now it's come full circle in another way: Morgans is consulting for a team coached by one of his former players. Central's head coach, Tim McGorry, was on one of Morgans's championship teams. Another one of his former Parkland players is pacing on the sidelines by the Vikings' bench. Jamie, clad in khaki shorts and the dark polo shirt worn by Central Catholic's coaching staff, is the team's defensive line coach. A baseball cap sits backward on his head and headphones are in place to hear instructions from the coaching box.

To see two former players on the Central Catholic coaching staff affirms the importance of relationships in football as far as Jim Morgans is concerned. He recounts running into Jamie the first time at a Central Catholic practice earlier in the fall.

"It's like we never were away from each other. I knew he was coaching there, but I saw him, and we met in the weight room. I hadn't seen him in probably a year," Morgans says. "Then I saw him, and we had time to talk about football . . . and everything else, and we spent a half hour just talking to each other."

As it is for his former high school coach, football remains central in Jamie's life. He works a day job in marketing and sales for Gatorade, a role that keeps him in contact with people in the athletic field. But outside of work, coaching football and umpiring softball occupies much of his time. After graduating from William & Mary, he returned to the Lehigh Valley, coached for a year at Parkland and then joined the coaching staff at Moravian College. He took a break from coaching and was a football referee. "But I got tired of being yelled at," he says chuckling. He welcomed the chance to return to coaching at Central Catholic. Football, he says, is more than a game.

Married in 2015, he and his wife, Alyssa, welcomed their son in 2017. The baby is also James—the sixth James Pagliaro. "We're going to call him JP," Jamie explains. Among the first pictures of the newborn was one of him posed slumbering cozily near Jamie's Tribe football helmet from William & Mary.

"My wife didn't know what she was getting into when she married me. She'd never been around a football player like me," Jamie says. If he isn't coaching, he's watching the game—high school games on Friday, college matches on Saturday, and the pros on Sundays. "It's more than just a sport. You bleed football. You enjoy the little things people don't see about the game." He explains that people who haven't played the sport or embraced it as a passionate fan don't "realize the intricacies and depth of the game." And there's something else that he thinks sets football apart: "There's a camaraderie in football that you don't get in any other sport," Jamie says.

He acknowledges that what happened to his friend Owen affected him. But it has not diminished his love for football. "It doesn't affect the way I view the sport or the lessons I learned from playing it," he says.

Jamie isn't the only former Trojan to become a coach. Mike Fay, who came reluctantly to the game as a middle schooler, now coaches the middle school team in the Southern Lehigh School District, just south of Allentown. He teaches high school English and started out coaching the junior varsity team but took a step back to teach the younger boys. It will allow him to spend more time with his growing family that includes a spunky toddler, Penelope, and an infant son, River. He found that the six- to seven-day-a-week demands on high school coaches—practices, games, analyzing film—left little time for anything else. Before making the move to middle-school coaching, he consulted Bob Steckel, the guy who coached him in middle school, for advice. Mike laughs, remembering that he was complaining about some of his players during their conversation. Coach Steckel, his hair now gray, reminded Mike of his own beginnings.

"And he said, 'Don't forget, Michael, that you got a scholarship and you were that fat kid crying on the sideline because we had you run,'" Mike says. "And I said, 'You know, you're absolutely right.'"

Armed with Steckel's advice, fall afternoons find Mike back on the sidelines, a small portable white board close at hand to illustrate plays. After years of being a Parkland Trojan, Mike is coaching the Southern Lehigh Spartans. It's another thing that doesn't change about football: team names on every level of play continue to honor history's most valiant warriors, fearless in battle, willing to die with honor. At the Southern Lehigh stadium, homemade signs near the entrance to the locker room offer inspiration from the sport's history. There is advice from George Halas, legendary Chicago Bears coach: "Nobody who ever gave his best regretted it." Or words from Pittsburgh Steelers Hall of Fame quarterback Terry Bradshaw: "When you've got something to prove, there's nothing greater than a challenge." Or some thoughts from a Pennsylvania native, quarterback Joe Namath: "Football is an honest game. It's true to life. It's a game about sharing. It's a team game. So is life."

So much about the game is rooted in its traditions. But Mike and other coaches also have new rules to follow. Concussion protocols, now an accepted part of play, govern when players must leave a game and when they will be allowed to return to play. A team physician stands ready in the stands to evaluate players, should the need arise. Although it wasn't part of his own experience as a player, Mike has adapted to the new rules.

Coaching younger players follows a time-honored pattern of skill building and mentoring. During a hard-fought game against an undefeated team from Catasauqua, Pennsylvania, Mike calls a player over after a play to review what happened and discuss what might have worked better. He illustrates his point on the white board. When he speaks to a member of the team, Mike looks him in the eye, often with a hand on his shoulder. This is a chance to start players, however enthusiastic or reluctant they might be at thirteen, on the path to playing football for the next eight years or more. Although Mike was not enthusiastic at the start of his own playing career, he credits the sport with bringing him to where he is today. "It was obviously the best thing that ever happened to me in terms of community and friendship and college scholarship and job and coaching. It's a huge part of my identity now," Mike says.

Bob Steckel says he's honored that Mike asked him for advice about coaching. "I told him, 'I'm so proud of you for asking these things. The fact that you're willing to listen to what I had to say means a lot,'" Bob says. He's retired after coaching for twenty-five years—seventeen at the middle-school level—but still volunteers with Parkland's middle school team. Like Jim Morgans, he's found that it's not easy to walk away from a sport that's been the thread running through the fabric of his life. And like they are for Morgans, relationships are perhaps the most significant part of what football has meant to him.

"I tell our kids all time: Your best friends are going to come from the locker room," Steckel says. "Our culture is so individualistic. People are taught to step on other people to get ahead. In football, it's different. It's the consummate team sport. We don't experience that in this culture. Individualism is what we aspire to. It leaves you feeling hollow."

His own life is proof that football breeds lasting friendships. As he prepares to leave on a fishing trip with former teammates, he notes, "We've been the best of friends since ninth grade. In spite of your warts, they still love you."

Since Owen's death and CTE diagnosis, Steckel has concluded that the brain injury must have been a factor in his former player's suicide. It's the only explanation for the way Owen ended his life—an action that seemed so out of character for the young man who was both fearless and feared on the gridiron. Owen's old locker at Parkland remains a shrine to his memory, one that Steckel created when he died, filled with his old jersey, newspaper clippings, and team photos. His loss has led Steckel to ponder the physical damage that can happen on the field. "Is there a negative physical aspect?" he asks. "Yes. Look at me: I have this wrong with me, I've got that wrong with me. I know it's because of football. I've had a knee replacement, knee surgery, back problems. But I wouldn't change anything. Next to my family, it's one of the most important things in my life."

Because he knows his body has paid the price for his love of the game, and because he loved Owen Thomas, Steckel made a decision: when he dies, his brain and spinal cord will go to the CTE brain bank at Boston University to be used in CTE research.

||||||||||||

During his time at Penn, Jake Peterson had developed a relationship with Andy Reid, then head coach of the Philadelphia Eagles, and with it came the opportunity to play professionally. For a player like him, it would fulfill the dream of a lifetime. He was preparing to participate in off-season workouts known as optional team activities with the pros when he tore his Achilles tendon. Characteristically drawing on his Mormon faith, Jake said, "Looking at the spiritual side of things, it was a massive blessing. It woke me up. It made me realize that maybe I need to look at something besides this game."

It wasn't an easy transition when he stepped away from something that had defined him since he was a kid.

"I had to learn to answer the questions 'Who am I? What do I do?' Before, it was 'I'm Jake Peterson. I play football,'" he recalls. "Now I'm Jake Peterson. Period. It was a huge loss of identity."

Since graduating from college, he's built a career in the fitness industry in California, gotten married, and become a father to a daughter in fall 2019. He remains active in his Mormon faith. Even watching football games on weekends has taken a backseat to other interests. For example, on Sundays he's busy with his church. If he's not working, he prefers to spend time with his wife. The years playing football seem very far away.

"For decades, [football] was my number one priority in life. It influenced the way I slept, the way I ate. From high school on, it was my top priority. That wasn't fun. I wish I had enjoyed things a little bit more. Ultimately it just ends up being a game."

He's not the only former Quaker to turn his back on football. After graduating with a degree in biomedical engineering, Daniel Lipschutz was living the life twenty-somethings dream of having. He had a good job, an apartment in Hoboken, New Jersey, and a lot of free time to socialize. "I started realizing my job wasn't challenging enough and it didn't leave me very fulfilled or energized," Daniel says. He left his engineering job in 2015 to travel, spending time in Bangladesh and other countries. A mechanical engineering and design class taken in his last year at Penn had sparked a long-forgotten interest in drawing. Eventually he returned to Philadelphia, establishing himself as a freelance graphic designer, muralist, and teaching artist. Working with a mural arts program in the city has given him "amazing opportunities," he says. It's caused him to focus in a way that reminds him of the days when he first learned to kick a football. He likens the focus required to learn to be a place kicker with the focus he brings to creating art.

"That was tapping into a similar part of my brain that hadn't been tapped since those early months of playing football," Daniel says.

He was ambivalent about his beloved Philadelphia Eagles' 2017 Super Bowl. It prompted him to write a long, thoughtful statement on Facebook.

"Football has provided so many benefits to my life. Some of my old teammates are still living their NFL dreams today, and it's been thrilling watching them manifest their careers. But the current state of the game that I once loved is breaking my heart," He says. "I can't watch without thinking about Owen and wishing he were still here. I'm in a strange place, having played the one position largely devoid of any chance of head trauma. I don't have to worry about my own brain in this regard, but I can't help thinking about my friends."

Although many of the football boys experienced changes in their transition from college to adult life, perhaps the most significant change came with fatherhood. Raucous parties were replaced by baby showers and get-togethers for a child's first birthday. Marc Quilling was the first to become a father with the birth of Chase Owen in 2012. His second child, a daughter named Alivia, arrived in 2016. His pictures on social media are now likely to be shots of family camping trips or trick-or-treating at Halloween. Mike Fay, who once protected Marc's blind side on the football field, posts pictures of his wife, Stephanie, little Penelope, and baby River on afternoon trips to the pumpkin patch or visits to Santa Claus at a Christmas tree farm.

Jamie Pagliaro and his wife, Alyssa, have already brought their son, James, to William & Mary's Zable Stadium where Jamie played. When the couple announced that a second addition to their family slated to arrive in 2020 would be another boy, Jamie posted on social media, "We got two-fifths of an offensive line in the Pagliaro household!" The baby, whom they named Brady, was born January 2, 2020.

For those who are the fathers of boys, there is the inevitable question of whether their sons will play football. At one time, Owen's friends would have said that the question is not "if," but "when." The answer is not as clear now. They all agree that they have no regrets about playing. CTE—which, with every new research finding, appears to have been a significant factor in their friend's death—has not tarnished the game for them. The shared bond with other men who love football made it worth the risk. The brotherhood formed around hours in the weight room, the shared discipline of early morning runs, and the joy of Friday nights under the lights or crisp fall Saturdays in the stadium is an indelible part of their lives.

"It meant so much, including building character for me and my friends," Marc Quilling says. "High school football for me was one of the best times of my life, from the point of view of the brotherhood I had from playing the game. The friends I had and the coaches I had were some of my best friends." He supports the idea of his son playing the game "100 percent." Marc acknowledges that flag football is the best way for the youngest players to begin building skills.

Jamie agrees, saying he is open to the caveat that the youngest players should not play tackle. "If they want to set an age limit for when they start playing contact, I'm fine with that," he says without hesitation. He also thinks better equipment should be required for youth football.

Although they all remain passionate about football, the reality of Owen's CTE diagnosis and the mounting body of research around the traumatic brain injury has changed their attitudes about some aspects of the game.

Owen's brother Morgan admits that he has tempered his passion for games filled with cracking hits. "ESPN had a show where they would show highlights of people getting smashed. I used to love it. Now when I see those violent hits, those violent collisions, I don't know what I was thinking." His own style of play, he concedes, probably put him at risk for CTE. "I used to love, when I played football, that I would have all the different facemask marks on my helmet," he says, adding, "I led with my head a lot." With that admission comes a question: Why does he not exhibit any CTE symptoms when Owen did? "Owen and I are brothers and we are blood. How was it so prevalent in his brain? How can I be functioning relatively normally while he seemed to have symptoms as early as he did?" Both Morgan and his father pledged their brains to the Boston University brain bank, hoping that it may help to find reasons why heredity appeared to single out Owen.

Nevertheless, he will allow his son Tanner to play, quickly adding, "If he wants to play." And he adds a proviso: "But probably not before seventh grade. That's when I started playing. That's middle school. And maybe not until he's a freshman. He's definitely not playing peewee football. There are so many other sports you can play where you can develop skills. I'm glad we have the research that we have now. And we know, of course, that this is bad for a kid. Their brains are still developing. There's no way kids should be out there banging their heads at that age."

While Mike Fay keenly misses his friend, Owen's death and CTE diagnosis have not dimmed his passion for football. He enjoys coaching and still likes watching the game. On Sundays, his social media feed displays pictures of his son and daughter decked out in kid-size Philadelphia Eagles gear. His son, River, had a replica of a Parkland Trojans jersey before he was six months old. Nevertheless, on some days he feels ambivalent as he contemplates the risks he was exposed to by playing the sport.

"I'm on the fence: my best friend perhaps died because of that. I probably had fifty concussions in my life. I was a lineman, I was smacking heads in every single play," Mike says, savoring the hyperbole. He is quiet for a moment, his brown eyes thoughtful. "But I would have to say, overall, no, it hasn't changed the way I coach football. Part of me thinks that if playing the game you love and having passion is going to somehow lead to that, maybe having that. . . . is worth it, you know?"

Luke DeLuca thinks of Owen frequently. He sells commercial real estate in a territory that includes the Lehigh Valley as well as Bucks and Montgomery Counties. When Luke puts gas in his car, he will fill the tank until the charge hits forty cents. Forty was Owen's Penn Quakers number. "It's another way of remembering him. That way, I'm remembering him a couple of times a week," Luke says.

He says that if he has sons, he'll allow them to play football when they are older, provided that they can observe better rules to protect their heads. Although he doesn't worry about it, he also knows he put himself at risk for CTE. "I feel like, had I known that head collisions could have that effect, I would have changed the way I hit people," Luke says. "I played a position where I hit people. Very often I would hit someone with my head when I could have used my shoulder."

Even with the advantage of hindsight, there's no question that he would still play football. He loved it. One question brings him up short.

"I wonder what Owen's decision would be about playing, if he had known what would happen." All of Owen's friends pondered the question at some point after his death. Among them, there is a sense of fatalism, a belief that Owen would not, *could not*, have been dissuaded from playing football.

Luke is no different. It takes him less than ten seconds to answer.

"I bet he would play."

EPILOGUE

THE BEIGE AND GRAY BUILDING with aluminum siding, tucked behind the VA Medical Center in Boston's Jamaica Plain neighborhood, could be mistaken for a maintenance building. There's a sign nearby that says motorcycles can be stored. A neighboring building has an open garage bay, and a backhoe is visible inside. It feels like a place frequented by workmen. Except the building with no sign and no visible identification has a doorbell like the kind you find on a house. Ring it and the gray metal door is opened by a lab technician.

Stepping inside, there's a large poster hanging in the corridor, the kind that researchers and scientists use to present their findings at conferences and research symposiums. This one has images of brain tissue stained brown. The brain belonged to Owen Thomas. Nearly ten years after Owen's death, his is the first illustrated case visitors see on entering this nondescript building housing the VA-BU-CLF Brain Bank. Back in 2010, when Ann McKee studied Owen's brain and found he had CTE, there were a couple of dozen brains in the brain bank. Now it houses more than seven hundred. New brains arrive every week, processed in this building in a deliberately obscure location that keeps the high-profile research out of the public eye.

The story of Owen's case lingers beyond the brain bank's walls. In 2018, journalist Malcolm Gladwell would devote an episode of his podcast, *Revisionist History*, to revisiting Owen's story and the issue of CTE and college football. In opening the episode, titled "Burden of Proof," Gladwell says, "This episode is about Owen Thomas, a young man I never had the chance to meet. About what happened to him and why we should not forget about him."

He also would pose the question: "What level of proof do we need about the harmfulness of some activity before we act?" In the podcast, Tom Thomas, Kathy Brearley, and their son Morgan tell the stories they had told so many times already: how Owen had lived the life of a warrior until he crumbled at the end of his junior year at Penn. Gladwell would emphasize, "When I said at the beginning that we shouldn't forget about Owen Thomas, I'm talking about this: that we shouldn't forget that he went from clarity and purpose to failing everything."

Ann McKee also has not forgotten Owen. Like Gladwell, she had never met him but, even after hundreds of cases, Owen's is one that she still cites in presentations and mentions in interviews. A decade after his death, in her office on the twelfth floor of the VA hospital, the stacks of stained slides have grown. The specimens reflect her relentless search for the truth about what happens to brains when athletes and military veterans are subjected to impacts that human beings aren't supposed to sustain on a regular basis.

Just as CTE research has evolved and changed, so has its most visible researcher. McKee is different than she was when she began this research. Some differences are visible in her office. There's a lot less Green Bay Packers memorabilia, although she still has a framed *Sports Illustrated* cover showing Vince Lombardi hoisted on his players' shoulders following his last win as Green Bay coach. But now it is a counterpoint to another cover from the same magazine hanging below it, this one with the headline: "Concussions . . . The hits that are changing the game . . . And the hits no one is noticing."

On the wall facing her desk is evidence that the credibility she was often denied early in her research has, nearly a decade later, finally been bestowed. There's the framed cover of *The Boston Globe Magazine* from 2017 announcing McKee as its Bostonian of the Year. That was the year before *Time* magazine named her one of its hundred Most Influential People. Beside the *Globe* cover is a color picture of former New England Patriot Aaron Hernandez, another athlete whose brain came under her microscope after his death and who was found to have CTE. The Hernandez picture was a gift from a *Boston Globe* reporter. A third framed article from *The New York Times* about women CTE researchers completes the trio.

In addition to recognition from mainstream media, McKee has received honors from her peers in the medical community: the 2018 Henry Wisniewski Lifetime Achievement Award from the Alzheimer's Association and election to the National Academy of Medicine.

But the truth is that, by 2018, McKee did not need the recognition. She knows unequivocally that her research is both valid and important. The criticisms do not affect her in the way they once did. "You stop caring about making people happy. As a woman, you know, we're all trained to be pleasers. And also, I'm very conscious that I was raised to be considerate and conscious and appreciative of how the other person is. . . . And so those situations were very hard for me, originally," McKee says. "They're not pleasant now, but I really don't care what people think of me. It's like, look: If I cared, I would've stopped a long time ago. So think what you like. I'm going to do what I feel compelled to do and I'm not losing any steam."

Although she's over sixty, she has no plans to retire. "I won't ever be done. I mean, I don't think this will come to conclusion in my lifetime. I can't stop now."

The findings from the CTE research could open the door to understanding more about other neurodegenerative diseases—a dream for McKee. "I can't imagine a cold stop, because it's just too much part of you. . . . We're so crazy committed at this point. How could we stop?" She pauses, and there is a trace of amusement in her blue eyes. "So—the reason I haven't retired: old scientists die on the job, don't you know that?"

|||||||||||

Like Ann McKee and Malcolm Gladwell, I'd never met Owen Thomas. I'd attended the church where his father was pastor and, when Owen died, I joined the memorial page established by his friends on Facebook. The stories shared there had convinced me that there was a story that needed to be told. I was compelled to find out who this young, redheaded football player had been and why so many friends, teammates, teachers, even casual acquaintances felt forever changed because they knew him. His CTE diagnosis was just one aspect of a story that centered on the relationships among young men on a football team. I contemplated writing that story for months before I began work on it on September 30, 2012—Owen's birthday.

But before I started, I went to see Tom Thomas at Union United Church of Christ. I was about to begin interviewing people about Owen and I wanted him to know before he heard secondhand. Given his role as a minister, it felt like I was seeking his blessing for the project. I sat in his office, the cemetery where Owen was buried visible over his shoulder, and told him I wanted to write about his son. For the briefest moment, Tom's face registered surprise. He paused for a minute, thoughtfully considering my reasons for writing about Owen and his friends. In a few minutes, in his gentle and soft-spoken way, he was suggesting which of Owen's friends should be interviewed for the book. Later there would be several long interviews with him and his wife, Kathy. Their courage and faith inspired me. We would run into each other at the fundraisers his sons' friends held in Owen's memory. He'd ask me how it was going. He supported the project, even when it seemed to stretch on indefinitely. He supported it, even when it meant that he had to contact the Philadelphia coroner for a copy of his son's autopsy because I needed it and only a family member could request it. The autopsy was sent to Tom and Kathy's home and I went there on a spring Saturday to get it. We spent some time sitting on his deck talking about it. "I read this," he said, as he handed the envelope from the coroner to me. "I'd never seen this before," he added quietly, as if I would be surprised that a parent had not read their child's autopsy after his tragic death by suicide.

|| | | | | | | | | | | |

On a Saturday morning in April 2019, I got off the elevator on the seventh floor at Lehigh Valley Hospital-Cedar Crest in suburban Allentown and walked through the automatic doors into wing 7A. It was quiet and I could hear my rubber-soled shoes scuffing the beige tile floor. The low murmur of subdued voices from visitors in the rooms along the corridor accompanied me as I looked for room 4. Walking through its door, I headed for the bed by the window. Tom Thomas was propped up, graying hair tousled, an IV in his arm and a hospital gown visible above the bedclothes. Get-well artwork from his two grandchildren hung on the wall, next to a University of Virginia Cavaliers jersey hung to celebrate his alma mater's win in college basketball's Final Four. A sports program was on the television, but the sound was muted. Tom's eyes were closed and I hesitated, reluctant to wake him. But I had nearly two hundred pages of a manuscript under my arm, and its weight reminded me that I was there for a reason: although we'd talked about it together for nearly a decade, Tom had never read any of the book that I'd written about his son.

Barely a month before my hospital visit, members of his former congregation learned that Tom was sick with what was described as a serious health issue. At the beginning of April, word came that he'd been admitted to the hospital. Not long after, on Caring Bridge, an online site that people use to give updates about seriously ill friends and family members, Kathy began posting updates about his condition. She explained that

Tom's lung cancer, which had necessitated removing one-third of his right lung in 2013, had metastasized to his brain. Although he had been declared cancer free in 2018, by September of that year he was not feeling himself. On March 16, 2019, an MRI was done to determine the cause of pressure behind his right eye. It showed he had three brain tumors—one pressing on the optic nerve and two on the frontal or temporal lobes. His condition deteriorated rapidly after the diagnosis and he was admitted to the hospital on March 28.

Pastor Kris Snyder-Samuelson, who succeeded him as senior pastor at Union United Church of Christ, had asked if I'd go to the hospital and read him part of the book.

Standing in his hospital room, I said his name once—"Pastor Tom"—and his eyes opened. "It's Vicki Mayk." I came around to the side of his bed and touched his hand. "I wanted to see you. Do you remember that I told you that the book about Owen is going to be published?" I'd emailed him with the news in January. He looked uncertain, so I repeated the information. It seemed to refresh his memory.

"Pastor Kris thought I should come and read you a preview. Would you like that?"

He nodded and I began reading. "Owen Thomas entered the world screaming . . ."

||||||||||||

Tom Thomas died on May 17, 2019. His memorial service was held a week later, at Union United Church of Christ. Before the service, Tom's cremated remains were in Memorial Hall at the church—the site of Sunday coffee hours after services and the room where he'd led many vacation bible school programs and gatherings at the church. Surrounding the simple box that held his remains was a small collection of objects that reflected Tom's interests: a green ministerial stole, a University of Virginia baseball cap, a hammer, and his worn brown work boots. A single rose was on the table by the box.

I waited in a long line to pay my condolences. Kathy stood in a dark dress near her husband's ashes, her long hair pulled back. Her son Morgan was nearby with his wife, Brittany. Kathy gestured toward Tom's remains. "Whoever thought it would end like this?" she said. "What an epilogue." She turned to me, her deep blue eyes steady. "You know, we harvested Tom's brain to send to Boston."

It would go where his son's brain had gone, to Ann McKee's research lab.

At Tom's memorial service, one of the people eulogizing him would speak of the decision to donate Tom's brain as an act that reflected his character. The Reverend Dr. Larry Pickens, ecumenical director of the Lehigh Conference of Churches, had worked with Tom on its interfaith committee, promoting understanding among the many faith traditions in the community. But Pickens said that unexpectedly they found common ground in another way: around the experience of football. "We both shared the experience of being college football linemen. He, of course, was in a major college program at the University of Virginia. I played for a Division III school. But as we talked about our football careers, he began to tell me the story about the death of his son, Owen, a lineman at the University of Pennsylvania. A twenty-one-year-old junior who was diagnosed with CTE—chronic traumatic encephalopathy, a disease that's generally attributed to repetitive head trauma," Pickens said. "And as Tom talked, I stopped him. I said, 'Wait a minute Tom. I know this story.'

"And the reason I knew the story is I realized that it was one of the vignettes shared in the book written by Sheryl Sandberg, *Option B: Facing Adversity, Building Resilience and Finding Joy*. I had read that book just before having this conversation with Tom. And it was in that moment that I developed a connection and a bond with Tom Thomas. It was on the human level that I encountered Tom. It was in looking through the crucible of his pain and faith that I began to understand the depth of this man. He was a man of conviction and faith."

Noting that Tom had decided to make a difference after Owen's death by placing himself on the brain registry at Boston University CTE Center, to study his brain as part of research that will help others, Pickens added, "That is what social justice is. It's making a difference with your life in order to help others."

Following Tom's memorial service, those attending followed the same path that they had walked nine years before at Owen's funeral, leaving the church from a side door and cutting through a parking lot to the adjacent graveyard. Tom was laid to rest near Owen. Just as it had been nine years before, it was a perfect spring day in May. The sun shone in a nearly cloudless sky. Leaves trembled in the soft breeze. And at noon, the chimes in the tall, white steeple of Union United Church of Christ tolled a melody that spilled over the surrounding countryside.

BIBLIOGRAPHICAL NOTE

WHENEVER I HAVE NOT included an endnote, the quotations, background, and descriptions of persons, places, or events were drawn from hours of interviews conducted for the book. The following are the interviews and the dates on which they occurred. Except where I have noted interviews done by phone, all interviews were conducted in person. All interviews lasted an hour or longer.

Michael Alosco, MD: April 11, 2019 (phone)

Abbie and Jess Benner: February 23, 2013, and July 27, 2014

Jamie Berkowitz: February 23, 2015, and October 11, 2017 (phone)

Rev. Kathy Brearley and Rev. Thomas N. Thomas: May 26, 2013, and September 5, 2016

Diane Cortazzo: April 13, 2013 (phone)

Luke DeLuca: January 30, 2018, and September 9, 2019 (phone)

Luke DeLuca and Emily Toth (DeLuca): June 9, 2013

Irina Levin and Kristen Dota: January 11, 2015

Kristen Dota: August 17, 2014, and November 25, 2017

Mike Fay: November 17, 2012; December 31, 2014; October 21, 2017; and April 20, 2019

Adam Grant: October 16, 2017 (phone)

Cory Smull Hausman: March 8, 2016 (phone)

Ryan Hulmes: June 24, 2016

Daniel Lipschutz: March 31, 2016 (phone); October 15, 2016 (phone); November 26, 2017; September 17, 2019

Dave Macknet: November 24, 2017 (phone)

Katharine Mayk: June 29, 2019

Ann McKee, MD: June 9, 2015, and April 4, 2019

Jim Morgans: May 9, 2015; June 2, 2019; and October 12, 2019

Jennifer Mueller: November 20, 2017 (phone)

Katie Novak: October 7, 2012 (phone)

Christopher Nowinski, PhD: April 4, 2019

Jamie Pagliaro: April 18, 2013; June 13, 2019; and August 18, 2019 (phone)

Jake Peterson: July 24, 2016, and August 27, 2019 (phone)

Morgan Potis, VA-BU-CLF Brain Bank: April 4, 2019

Marc Quilling: October 21, 2012; November 6, 2014; August 9, 2016; May 19, 2019; and August 7, 2019

Brian Reinert: January 4, 2013

Andy Roth: June 30, 2013

Lynette Smith: December 29, 2012

Rev. Kris Snyder-Samuelson: October 27, 2012

Bob Steckel: September 2, 2017, and August 6, 2019 (phone)

Kale Sweeney: July 12, 2014

Morgan Thomas: August 16, 2014, and January 28, 2018 (phone)

Rev. Thomas N. Thomas: May 8, 2015

Steve Yoder: April 17, 2013 (phone)

John Zaccaro: August 11, 2013

ACKNOWLEDGMENTS

ONE DAY IN 2010 I joined a memorial page on Facebook called "RIP Owen Thomas." On that page I met Owen Thomas through the posthumous stories told by his friends and family. This book is possible only because of the people who shared their stories and memories. I am most deeply indebted to the Thomas family. Owen's mother, Rev. Katherine Brearley; his brother Morgan; and his father, the late Rev. Thomas N. Thomas, trusted me with his story and gave freely of their time. Their courage, faith, and candor inspired me during the nearly ten years it took to me to write this book.

My heartfelt gratitude also extends to Owen's friends and teammates. This is their story, too, reflected in the fact that for several years the working title of the manuscript was *The Friends of Owen Thomas*. I owe so much to so many—but especially to Mike Fay and Marc Quilling. You were among my most trusted sources—but even more importantly, you cheered me on and never stopped believing that I really would finish this book. It's a tribute to your love for your friend Owen that you supported this project so faithfully for such a long time. Jamie Pagliaro, thank you for finding the time for more interviews when I circled back to you many years after we first talked. John Zaccaro, Andy Roth, and many other Parkland Trojans players from the 2002–2007 era—my thanks.

Although a book about football tends to be dominated by men, Owen's girlfriends and female friends were integral to capturing details of his life. Abbie and Jess Benner and Jamie Berkowitz—you were vital to this story. Kristen Dota, your stories about Owen informed so much of what I wrote. Thank you for the hours you spent talking to me.

Penn Quakers Luke DeLuca, Jake Peterson, Dave Macknet, and Daniel Lipschutz: my profound thanks for bringing Owen's Philadelphia years to life. Daniel—your generosity in accompanying me to a Quakers football game, when I'm sure you had other ways to spend a Saturday, and familiarizing me with the Penn campus was deeply appreciated.

Owen's Parkland football coaches Jim Morgans, Robert Steckel, and Ryan Hulmes helped me understand the relationship between high school coaches and their players. Coach Morgans, thanks for patiently walking me through coaching terminology and for bearing with my many requests. Equally important were Owen's Parkland School District teachers, whose stories illuminated Owen in the classroom as well as on the playing field. Thank you Lynette Smith, Cory Smull Hausman, Diane Cortazzo, and Steve Yoder.

Adam Grant, when you wrote about Owen in *Plan B*, I sped to a Barnes & Noble to buy the book and see what you had written. When I emailed you for an interview, your rapid response and the stories you shared breathed new life into my book.

I am grateful to Dr. Ann McKee and Christopher Nowinski, PhD, for their groundbreaking work related to CTE and head injuries. They generously granted me interviews before I had a contract for this book. It helped me to shape my early drafts. They generously gave me more of their valuable time as I finished the project. Gina DiGravio and the communications team at Boston University and the VA Medical Center were a writer's dream, responding to my queries quickly and professionally. Tyler Maland at the Concussion Legacy Foundation handled my requests related to Dr. Nowinski with professionalism and patience.

I am indebted to Dr. J. Michael Lennon, professor and cofounder of the Maslow Family Graduate Program in Creative Writing at Wilkes University, for the interest he took in this project. His support, encouragement, and belief in this book helped me stay the course. His thoughtful edits and guidance shaped my early drafts. Mike, you championed this project in a way that truly makes you my literary godfather. I also must thank my friend Dawn D'Aries Zera for her encouragement and for the role she played as a literary matchmaker when she told Mike about my book. Dawn, you are the definition of a literary citizen who supports her fellow writers.

This book is being published because of my intrepid agent Carolyn Savarese at Kneerim & Williams, who at times believed in it even more than I did. Thank you for your skillful editing and knowledgeable advice. Your savvy insights about the publishing industry always ensured that things were handled in my book's and my best interest. I appreciate your patience with me as a first-time book author.

I'm fortunate to have a great team at my publisher, Beacon Press. It's a great place for a book to find a home. Joanna Green, my editor, shared my vision for the book, walking with me through revision and helping to shape the manuscript with her insights and guidance. Thanks to others on the Beacon team—Susan Lumenello, Beth Collins, Margaret Field, Marcy Barnes, Emily Powers, and Alison Rodriguez—who shepherded it through the copyediting, production, and marketing process.

The faculty of the Maslow Family Graduate Creative Writing Program offered astute advice and encouragement. Particular thanks to Bonnie Culver, Kevin Oderman, Sara Pritchard, Kaylie Jones, Beverly Donofrio, Nancy McKinley, and Jeff Talarigo. What I learned from you can be seen on the pages of this book.

Rev. Kris Snyder-Samuelson at Union United Church of Christ, thank you for your prayers and support. I will always be grateful that you encouraged me to go to read some of the book to Tom Thomas before he died.

My writing group was my mainstay as I worked on the manuscript. Kelly Clisham, Jennifer Jenkins, Aurora Bonner, and

Francisco Tutella, your insights and feedback were invaluable. Francisco, your patience with my many text messages and your responses with the encouraging emojis always came at exactly the right time. Thank you for the chapter title: I owe you one. Writing can be a lonely business, but my wonderful, supportive friends—many of them fellow writers—ensured that I never felt alone. My best friend, Katherine Hamann, was always by my side, even when she was five hundred miles away. Above all, thanks for the laughter, Katrisha. Other friends encouraged me and offered advice during the long years I worked on this book. Tina Jarrett, Dawn Leas, Joy Smith Carey, Danielle Sewell, Heather Taylor, Mike Shoupe, Patti Naumann, Ginny Grove—I love you. Barbara J. Taylor, sincere thanks for sharing your experiences in bringing a book to print, and for dropping everything to have dinner and talk about titles.

My coworkers in the marketing communications department at Wilkes University made the "day job" fun. Gabrielle D'Amico, I was appreciative of your understanding when I needed to take vacation time to make a deadline. Few of us have the luxury of writing full-time and your flexibility made it possible for me to juggle deadlines on the job and on the book.

The first draft of this book was born at the Writer's Colony at Dairy Hollow in Eureka Springs, Arkansas. Thanks to the colony for providing me with a great working space, two weeks of uninterrupted writing time, and incredibly delicious food. I might never have written it without that start.

Finally, I close with my most personal note of thanks to my daughters, Katharine Mayk and Monica Mayk Berryhill. Monica, I won the stepmother lottery when you came into my life. Katti, you've been my "why" since the day you were born. My love for you both is at the center of all I do. Your support in the last three years, leading up to this book's publication, is what kept me going.

NOTES

PROLOGUE

1. "What Is CTE?," Frequently Asked Questions, Boston University CTE Center, https://www.bu.edu/cte/about/frequently-asked-questions.

2. Concussion Legacy Foundation, "CTE Resources: The Science of CTE," https://concussionfoundation.org/CTE-resources/science-of -CTE.

3. *Frontline*, "League of Denial: The NFL's Concussion Crisis, The *Frontline* Interviews," May 20, 2013, https://www.pbs.org/wgbh/pages /frontline/oral-history/league-of-denial.

4. Mark Fainaru-Wada and Steve Fainaru, *League of Denial: The NFL, Concussions, and the Battle for Truth* (New York: Three Rivers Press, 2013), 255.

CHAPTER ONE: GAME CHANGER

1. Parkland School District, "2018–2019 District Profile," https:// resources.finalsite.net/images/v1540994139/parklandsdorg/f55qyogodom 88q28sm4u/District-Profile-2018-19.pdf.

2. Andre D. Williams, "Easton-Parkland Highlights Football Card: Their PIAA Subregional One of Several Highlighting Local Teams," *Morning Call*, November 17, 2006, https://www.mcall.com/news/mc -xpm-2006-11-17-3699706-story.html.

3. Parkland Sports History, 1996 season and 2002 season, http:// www.parklandsportshistory.com/viewresults.asp?sportid=1.

4. NCAA, "2019 Estimated Probability of Competing in College Athletics," NCAA Research, https://ncaaorg.s3.amazonaws.com/research /pro_beyond/2019RES_ProbabilityBeyondHSFiguresMethod.pdf.

5. Michael Shapiro, "Fallen Giant," *Smithsonian*, February 2007, https://www.smithsonianmag.com/history/fallen-giant-144796136.

6. "Lawrence Taylor Remembers Joe Theismann's Brutal Injury," ESPN.com, November 18, 2016, https://www.espn.com/nfl/story/_/id /18074038/lawrence-taylor-remembers-joe-theismann-injury-seen-lot -worse-hits-nfl.

CHAPTER TWO: BIRTH OF A VIKING

1. Jimmy Stamp, "Leatherhead to Radio-head: The Evolution of the Football Helmet," *Smithsonian*, October 1, 2012, https://www.smithsonianmag.com/arts-culture/leatherhead-to-radio-head-the-evolution-of-the-football-helmet-56585562.

2. Bill Pennington, "The NFL's Incredible Shrinking Pads," *New York Times*, September 26, 2018, https://www.nytimes.com/2018/09/26/sports/football/nfl-pads-michael-bennett.html.

3. Dan Peterson, "How the NFL Football Got Its Shape," Live Science, September 8, 2010, www.livescience.com, https://www.livescience.com/32808-nfl-football-spheroid-origins.html.

4. Timothy Gay, *The Physics of Football: Discover the Science of Bone-Crunching Hits, Soaring Field Goals, and Awe-Inspiring Passes* (New York: It Books/Harper Collins, 2005), 59–62.

5. Fellowship of Christian Athletes, "Vision and Mission," https://www.fca.org/aboutus/who-we-are/vision-mission.

6. Mark Hyman, *The Most Expensive Game in Town: The Rising Cost of Youth Sports and the Toll on Today's Families* (Boston: Beacon Press, 2012), 56.

7. Hyman, *The Most Expensive Game in Town*, 8–9.

8. John J. Fox, "Trojans Thomas Is Tops: Parkland Running Back Is Lehigh Valley's No. 1 Scholar-Athlete," *Morning Call*, January 27, 1998, https://www.mcall.com/news/mc-xpm-1998-01-27-3188971-story.html.

9. National Federation of State High School Associations, "High School Athletics Participation History (1969–2008)" https://www.nfhs.org/media/1020206/hs_participation_survey_history_1969-2009.pdf.

CHAPTER THREE: SUITING UP

1. Pro Football Hall of Fame, "History of Football," https://www.profootballhof.com/football-history/history-of-football.

2. James Surowiecki, "Beautiful. Violent. American. The NFL at 100," *New York Times*, December 19, 2019, https://www.nytimes.com/2019/12/19/sports/football/nfl-100-violence-american-culture.html.

3. Kristen Shilton, "Overcoming Natural Fear of Contact Is an Important Early Step in Tackle Football," USA Football (blog), April 3, 2018, https://blogs.usafootball.com/blog/2623/overcoming-natural-fear-of-contact-is-an-important-early-step-in-tackle-football.

4. USA Football, "USA Football Tackling Systems," https://usafootball.com/development-training/tackling-systems.

5. Fainaru-Wada and Fainaru, *League of Denial*, 63–65.

6. Pro Football Hall of Fame, "Mike Webster's Enshrinement Speech," 1997 Hall of Fame Induction Ceremony, December 19, 2013, https://www.profootballhof.com/videos/mike-webster-enshrinement-speech.

CHAPTER FOUR: IN THE MIDDLE

1. John P. Martin, "Parkland High Target Date Extended to 1999," *Morning Call*, August 23, 1995, https://www.mcall.com/news/mc-xpm -1995-08-23-3048633-story.html.

2. National Federation of State High School Associations, "High School Athletics Participation History (1969–2008)."

3. Curry Quarterback Camp registration, http://curryqbcamp.org.

4. Sally Gigante, "Summer Sports Camps: Athletic Costs and Curveballs," MassMutual Blog, May 15, 2018, https://blog.massmutual.com /post/summer-sports-camps-athletic-costs-and-curveballs.

5. Jonathan D. Silver, "A Life Off-Center: Mike Webster's Battles," *Pittsburgh Post-Gazette*, October 17, 2014 (first published July 24, 1997), https://www.post-gazette.com/ae/movies/2014/10/17/A-life-off-center -Mike-Webster-s-battles/stories/201410090319.

6. Fainaru-Wada and Fainaru, *League of Denial*, 20–27.

7. Fainaru-Wada and Fainaru, *League of Denial*, 25–27.

8. Silver, "A Life Off-Center."

9. Fainaru-Wada and Fainaru, *League of Denial*, 148–57.

10. Fainaru-Wada and Fainaru, *League of Denial*, 158–65.

CHAPTER FIVE: FOOTBALL BOYS

1. Mark Maske, "New Rules on NFL Contact Haven't Altered Training Camps Much," *Washington Post*, August 13, 2011, https://www .washingtonpost.com/sports/redskins/new-rules-on-nfl-contact-havent -altered-training-camps-much/2011/08/13/gIQA68BvDJ_story.html.

2. Michelle Brutlag Hosick, "DI Council Votes to Eliminate Football Two-A-Days," April 14, 2017, http://www.ncaa.org/about /resources/media-center/news/di-council-votes-eliminate-football -two-days.

3. Keith Groller, "Jim Morgans Has Resigned as Parkland's Head Coach," *Morning Call*, March 29, 2016, https://www.mcall.com/sports /varsity/mc-jim-morgans-has-resigned-as-parkland-s-head-football -coach-20160329-story.html.

4. Gay, *The Physics of Football*, 59–62.

CHAPTER SIX: THUNDERCATS

1. Mary Ellen Alu, "Sniscak Appointed Parkland Superintendent," South Whitehall Patch, February 23, 2011, https://patch.com /pennsylvania/southwhitehall/sniscak-appointed-parkland -superintendent-gets-standing-ovation.

2. Marion Callahan and Andrew McGill, "Parkland Might Abolish Class Rank," *Morning Call*, June 17, 2009, https://www.mcall.com /news/mc-xpm-2009-06-17-4391585-story.html.

3. "Athletic Scouting and Recruiting Service Products," CHAMPs Inc., https://www.champs2.com/athletic-scouting-recruiting-service -products.

4. "2006 Parkland Trojans Season Highlights," video, Schaf Productions, Allentown, PA.

CHAPTER SEVEN: PENN PALS

1. University of Pennsylvania, "125 Years of Franklin Field," *Penn Today* news release, April 23, 2019, https://penntoday.upenn.edu/news /125-years-franklin-field.

2. Coach Bagnoli Central, PennAthletics.com, https://pennathletics .com/news/2016/6/27/5771ac12e4b0028e7235eda2_13149281330451 9656.aspx.

3. Jonathan Chait, "College Football Bans Wedge Blocking on Kickoffs," *New Republic*, April 16, 2010, https://newrepublic.com/article /74483/colle-football-bans-wedge-blocking-kickoffs.

4. "2009 Football: 40, Owen Thomas," PennAthletics.com, https:// pennathletics.com/sports/football/roster/owen-thomas/6907.

CHAPTER EIGHT: FOOTBALL FAMILY

1. Jane Leavy, "The Woman Who Would Save Football," Grantland .com, August 17, 2012, http://grantland.com/features/neuropathologist -dr-ann-mckee-accused-killing-football-be-sport-only-hope.

2. "Ann McKee, MD" Boston University Research: CTE Center, http://www.bu.edu/cte/about/leadership/ann-mckee-md.

3. Neil Swidey, "Bostonian of the Year 2017: Dr. Ann McKee," *Boston Globe Magazine*, December 13, 2017, https://www.bostonglobe.com /magazine/2017/12/13/mckee/TkYOjLJAmTcKrudoR6YMXJ/story.html.

4. Fainaru-Wada and Fainaru, *League of Denial*, 255–57.

5. Leavy, "The Woman Who Would Save Football."

6. Fainaru-Wada and Fainaru, *League of Denial*, 263–65.

7. Fainaru-Wada and Fainaru, *League of Denial*, 266–70.

8. Leavy, "The Woman Who Would Save Football."

9. Michele Monaco and Malissa Martin, "The Millennial Student: A New Generation of Learners," *Athletic Training Education Journal* 2, no. 2 (2007): 42–46.

CHAPTER NINE: PLAYING THROUGH THE PAIN

1. Julie Scelfo, "Suicide on Campus and the Pressure of Perfection," *New York Times*, July 17, 2015, https://www.nytimes.com/2015/08/02 /education/edlife/stress-social-media-and-suicide-on-campus.html.

2. Scelfo, "Suicide on Campus and the Pressure of Perfection."

3. "What Is CTE?," Boston University CTE Center.

4. "Autopsy Report and Death Investigation for Owen Thomas," Case No. 10–01705, Philadelphia Medical Examiner's Office, 2010.

5. "Autopsy Report and Death Investigation for Owen Thomas," Case No. 10–01705.

CHAPTER TEN: TESTIMONY

1. Fainaru-Wada and Fainaru, *League of Denial*, 198–201.

2. Chris Nowinski, "Can I Have Your Brain? The Quest for Truth on Concussion and CTE," filmed November 2017, TEDxBeaconStreet, https://www.ted.com/talks/chris_nowinski_can_i_have_your_brain_the _quest_for_truth_on_concussions_and_cte.

3. Alan Schwarz, "N.F.L. Asserts Greater Risks of Head Injury," *New York Times*, July 26, 2010, https://www.nytimes.com/2010/07/27/sports /football/27concussion.html.

4. Katherine Brearley, testimony before US House Committee on Education and Labor, 111th Cong., 2nd session, at hearing on H.R. 6172, Protecting Student Athletes from Concussions, September 23, 2010, https://www.govinfo.gov/content/pkg/CHRG-111hhrg58256 /html/CHRG-111hhrg58256.htm.

5. Brearley, testimony before US House Committee on Education and Labor.

6. Brearley, testimony before US House Committee on Education and Labor.

7. Brearley, testimony before US House Committee on Education and Labor.

8. Ann McKee, testimony before US Senate Committee on Commerce, Science, and Transportation, 112th Cong., 2nd session, at hearing on Concussions and the Marketing of Sports Equipment, October 19, 2011, https://www.commerce.senate.gov/2011/10/concussions-and -the-marketing-of-sports-equipment.

9. McKee, testimony before US Senate Committee on Commerce, Science, and Transportation.

10. Fainaru-Wada and Fainaru, *League of Denial*, 308–10.

11. Centers for Disease Control, National Center for Injury Prevention and Control, Division of Unintentional Injury Prevention, "Get a Heads Up on Concussions in Sports Policies: Information for Parents, Coaches, School and Sports Professionals," https://www.cdc.gov/headsup /pdfs/policy/headsuponconcussioninsportspolicies-a.pdf, accessed February 27, 2020.

CHAPTER ELEVEN: DIVINE PROVIDENCE

1. "Penn Football Beats Lafayette—Penn Post-Game Press Conference (Part 1)," *Daily Pennsylvanian*, September 1, 2010, YouTube, https://www.youtube.com/watch?v=J32heg65VVo.

2. "Penn Football Beats Lafayette."

3. Boston University School of Medicine, "Study: Hits, Not Concussions, Cause CTE," news release, January 18, 2018, https://www.bumc.bu.edu/busm/2018/01/18/study-hits-not-concussions-cause-cte.

CHAPTER TWELVE: CHANGING THEIR MINDS

1. Leavy, "The Woman Who Would Save Football."

2. Leavy, "The Woman Who Would Save Football."

3. "Super Bowl Ratings History (1967–present)," SportsMediaWatch.com, https://www.sportsmediawatch.com/super-bowl-ratings-historical-viewership-chart-cbs-nbc-fox-abc.

4. "NFL's 2013 Protocol for Players with Concussions," NFL.com, October 1, 2013, http://www.nfl.com/news/story/0ap2000000253716/article/nfls-2013-protocol-for-players-withconcussions.

5. Bill Bradley, "New NFL Rules: Crown-of-the-Helmet Change to Help Runner, Defender," NFL.com, September 5, 2013, http://www.nfl.com/news/story/0ap1000000238662/article/new-nfl-rules-crownofhelmet-change-to-help-runner-defender.

6. "NFL Implements Modifications to League's Concussion Protocol," NFL.com, December 24, 2017, http://www.nfl.com/news/story/0ap3000000897109/article/nfl-implements-modifications-to-leagues-concussion-protocol.

7. Ken Belson, "N.F.L. Agrees to Settle Concussion Suit for $765 Million," New York Times, August 29, 2013, https://www.nytimes.com/2013/08/30/sports/football/judge-announces-settlement-in-nfl-concussion-suit.html.

8. Nicky Bandini, "NFL Concussion Lawsuit Explained," Guardian, August 29, 2013, www.theguardian.com, https://www.theguardian.com/sport/2013/aug/29/nfl-concussions-lawsuit-explained.

9. Barry Wilner, "First Two Claims in NFL Concussion Settlement Total $9 Million," Associated Press, June 15, 2017, www.apnews.com, https://apnews.com/ecf1d852200e419dba91eeedcc1a57bd.

10. Ken Belson, "Ivy League to Limit Full-Contact Practices," New York Times, July 20, 2011, https://www.nytimes.com/2011/07/20/sports/ncaafootball/college-football-to-protect-players-ivy-league-to-reduce-contact.html.

11. "Ivy League Football Limits Full Contact Practices to Reduce Brain Injury," WHYY.org, July 21, 2011, www.whyy.org, https://whyy.org/articles/ivy-league-football-limits-full-contact-practices-to-reduce-brain-injury.

12. Craig Larson, "Ivy League Coaches Vote to Eliminate Full Contact Practices," Boston Globe, March 1, 2016, https://www.bostonglobe.com/sports/2016/03/01/ivy-league-coaches-vote-eliminate-full-contact-practices/LNMI86CGdFcnr51ONV7EFN/story.html.

13. Brian Burnsed, "Two-a-Day Q&A," *NCAA Champion Magazine*, July 19, 2017, www.ncaa.org, http://www.ncaa.org/champion/two-day-qa.

14. Jon Solomon, "Next Wave of Concussion Lawsuits Hits Conferences and, for Penn State, Schools," CBSSports.com, May 18, 2016, https://www.cbssports.com/college-football/news/next-wave-of -concussion-lawsuits-hits-conferences-and-for-penn-state-schools.

15. Ralph D. Russo, "Wave of Concussion Lawsuits to Test NCAA's Liability," AP News, February 7, 2019, https://APNews.com/4a4ed68e4 c3a426abc4e34606ae4a399.

16. Ken Belson and Alan Schwarz, "NFL Shifts on Concussions, and Game May Never Be the Same," March 15, 2016, *New York Times*, https://www.nytimes.com/2016/03/16/sports/nfl-concussions-cte -football-jeff-miller.html.

17. Sarah Rimer, "BU Researchers ID Possible Biomarker for Diagnosing CTE during Life," September 26, 2017, The Brink, http://www .bu.edu/articles/2017/diagnosing-cte-during-life.

18. Rimer, "BU Researchers ID Possible Biomarker for Diagnosing CTE during Life."

19. "Pop Warner Becomes First National Football Organization to Eliminate 3-Point Stance," PopWarner.com, February 28, 2019, http:// www.northwestpopwarner.org/news/2019/2/28/pop-warner-becomes -first-national-football-organization-to-eliminate-3-point-stance.

20. "National Practice Guidelines for Youth Tackle Football," USA Football.com, https://assets.usafootball.com/documents/practice -guidelines-youth.pdf.

21. "Number of Participants in Tackle Football in the U.S. from 2006 to 2018," Statista.com, August 9, 2019, statista.com/statistics /191658/participants-in-tackle-football-in-the-us-since-2006.

22. Ken Belson, Quoctrung Bui, Joe Drape, Rumsey Taylor, and Joe Ward, "Inside Football's Campaign to Save the Game," November 7, 2019, *New York Times*, https://www.nytimes.com/interactive/2019/11/08 /sports/falling-football-participation-in-america.html.

23. Ken Belson, "A Small Town Gave Up Tackle Football. It Came Storming Back," November 16, 2019, *New York Times*, https://www.ny times.com/2019/11/16/sports/youth-tackle-football-marshall-texas.html.

24. James Surowiecki, "Beautiful. Violent. American. The NFL at 100," *New York Times*, December 19, 2019.

25. Belson et al., "Inside Football's Campaign to Save the Game."

26. National Federation of State High School Associations, "High-School Athletics Participation History."

CHAPTER THIRTEEN: BUT NOT FORGOTTEN

1. PSFCA Hall of Fame, Class of 2019: Jim Morgans, https://big33 .org/psfca-hall-of-fame.